Praise for *Faster, Fewer, Better Emails*

"Email has become an omnipresent part of our professional and personal lives, so it's easy to treat it carelessly. This book is a great reminder of how email impacts not only your productivity but your professional reputation and even your security and that of your company. I'll be implementing Booher's strategies for me and my team."

—Brian Chase, Director, Future Vertical Lift Enterprise Alignment, Bell

"The incredible Dianna Booher has done it again, providing her unique wisdom and remarkable insights in the ways that only she can. Bravo!"

—Catherine Blades, Senior Vice President and Chief ESG and Communications Officer, Aflac

"Dianna Booher has written a must-read book for all those drowning in their email box. She provides practical advice and tips to master your email in today's digital world."

—Virginia Harnisch, Chief Compliance Officer/Managing Director, SMBC Capital Markets, Inc.

"Finally, a way out of email jail! Seriously, the strategies in this book can cut your email time in half—and improve communication flow."

—Kim Campbell, Senior Manager, Customer Advocacy, TXU Energy

"If you're a busy executive, have your team read and implement the strategies in this book. The productivity increases for you—and them—will be startling."

—Harold R. Loftin, Jr., Chief Legal Officer and General Counsel, GuideStone

"This book will open your eyes to a whole new way of thinking about email—its purposes, structure, improper uses, security risks, and productivity strategies."

—Marshall Goldsmith, author of the *New York Times* #1 bestselling *Triggers*, *Mojo*, and *What Got You Here Won't Get You There*

"Booher delivers another winner: practical strategies and tips to manage email volume, reduce the feeling of being perpetually overwhelmed, and promote clear communication."

—Brian Tracy, author of *Eat That Frog!*

"Dianna Booher is the master of her craft, the communicators' communicator, the go-to person for getting your point across memorably, efficiently, and effectively. With *Faster, Fewer, Better Emails*, she's delivered another winner and one you can put to use immediately. It's got a clear and concise format, practical tips, relevant examples, and a sound strategy for saving time and aggravation. Read this book now and earn immediate thanks from your colleagues and business from your customers."

—Jim Kouzes, coauthor of the bestselling *The Leadership Challenge* and Fellow, Doerr Institute for New Leaders, Rice University

"Practical strategies and tips to get real 24-7 communication gains from email and eliminate the productivity drain it all too often creates. . . . Another hit from Booher."

—Ralph D. Heath, former Executive Vice President, Lockheed Martin Corporation

FASTER,
FEWER,
BETTER
EMAILS

OTHER BUSINESS BOOKS BY DIANNA BOOHER

Communicate Like a Leader

Creating Personal Presence

What More Can I Say? (Perigee, 2015)

Communicate with Confidence (McGraw-Hill, 2011)

Booher's Rules of Business Grammar (McGraw-Hill, 2008)

The Voice of Authority (McGraw-Hill, 2007)

Great Personal Letters for Busy People (McGraw-Hill, 2006)

Your Signature Work (Tyndale House, 2004)

Your Signature Life (Tyndale House, 2003)

From Contact to Contract (Kaplan, 2003)

Speak with Confidence! (McGraw-Hill, 2002)

E-Writing (Pocket Books, 2001)

Good Grief, Good Grammar (Ballantine, 1989)

FASTER, FEWER, BETTER EMAILS

Manage the Volume,
Reduce the Stress,
Love the Results

Dianna Booher

BK
Berrett–Koehler Publishers, Inc.

Berrett-Koehler Publishers, Inc.
1333 Broadway, Suite 1000
Oakland, CA 94612-1921
Tel: (510) 817-2277
Fax: (510) 817-2278
www.bkconnection.com

ORDERING INFORMATION
Quantity sales. Special discounts are available on quantity purchases by corporations, associations, and others. For details, contact the "Special Sales Department" at the Berrett-Koehler address above.
Individual sales. Berrett-Koehler publications are available through most bookstores. They can also be ordered directly from Berrett-Koehler: Tel: (800) 929-2929; Fax: (802) 864-7626; www.bkconnection.com.
Orders for college textbook / course adoption use. Please contact Berrett-Koehler: Tel: (800) 929-2929; Fax: (802) 864-7626.

Distributed to the U.S. trade and internationally by Penguin Random House Publisher Services.

Berrett-Koehler and the BK logo are registered trademarks of Berrett-Koehler Publishers, Inc.

Printed in the United States of America

Berrett-Koehler books are printed on long-lasting acid-free paper. When it is available, we choose paper that has been manufactured by environmentally responsible processes. These may include using trees grown in sustainable forests, incorporating recycled paper, minimizing chlorine in bleaching, or recycling the energy produced at the paper mill.

Cataloging-in-Publication Data is available at the Library of Congress.
ISBN: 978-1-5230-8512-5

First Edition

25 24 23 22 21 20 19   10 9 8 7 6 5 4 3 2 1

Produced by Wilsted & Taylor Publishing Services
Text designer: Michael Starkman, Wilsted & Taylor
Cover designer: Susan Malikowski, DesignLeaf Studio

Contents

Introduction

I do love email. Wherever possible I try to communicate asynchronously. I'm really good at email.

—**ELON MUSK,** founder and CEO of SpaceX,
cofounder and CEO of Tesla and Neuralink

Lorenzo, a colleague of mine, emailed me to say he needed to find a regional distributor and asked if I'd put the word out to my network. The "ideal distributor" would build a sales team, receive a commission of regional sales, and have an equity position in the company.

Culling my contact list, I emailed him a few prospects for consideration. He connected with all three candidates by phone. Bingo, one showed immediate interest and had all the right credentials—that is, until Lorenzo and the potential distributor began to exchange emails.

Lorenzo emailed detailed information about the distributorship to the candidate, Amy, and asked her to respond with her plans to grow the region. Amy sent back a cryptic email from her smartphone:

> Interested , , , traveling very excited sending more when back in office.

Two weeks later, Amy followed up with another cryptic email. It, too, sounded as though she'd emailed while dashing through an airport security checkpoint, with an unpunctuated stream-of-thought message, grammatical errors and misspellings, and incomplete information.

That's when Lorenzo forwarded Amy's two emails to me with this question:

"Am I overreacting about this person's ability to communicate? Read her emails (below) and tell me if I can afford to partner with someone like this to represent our company at a senior level? Although she'll eventually be managing and not selling, at the beginning, she will have direct client contact. Can I trust this person to communicate with clients?"

I read the email string Lorenzo forwarded to me. Candidate Amy's excitement about the distributorship potential came through strongly. But her emails looked as if they'd been written by someone just learning the language. In addition to the errors, she rambled on with vague generalities, falling short on specifics.

"Maybe it's a fluke," I responded to Lorenzo. "Maybe she's not feeling well. If she has all the right sales and marketing experience and management credentials, why don't you tell her bluntly how important writing is to the partnership. . . . Just see what she says."

So Lorenzo tried that approach. He mentioned his concerns about her writing, but said he was otherwise thrilled with the growth plans they'd originally discussed on the phone.

Amy's reply? Another rambling, error-filled email.

Lorenzo gave up and moved on to the next candidate. To put it in his words: "I have too much invested in my brand and business to have a distributor who can't compose a simple, clear email!"

CONSIDER IMAGE, SECURITY, LIABILITY

Email matters NOT just because of credibility and clarity. Email also poses security risks and legal liabilities. All that adds up either to big pluses or big minuses, depending on how well your email works for or against you.

For more than three decades, I've been reading emails to and from people at all levels in client organizations across myriad industries—hundreds of thousands of emails. My firm analyzes why the original versions don't work and why the edited versions get better responses.

And the most revealing thing in our work? "Impact" stories. The lawsuits based on sloppy wording. The loss of clients because of insensitive remarks. Inaccurate payments caused by missing information. Frustration and missed deadlines because of inconsistency in filing important attachments.

This entire book could be a collection of such blunders and their associated career and organizational costs. But that would only cause more stress for the reader. Instead, this book aims to make email work FOR you. The goal is to fix these problems!

STOP THE STRESS AND PRODUCTIVITY DRAIN

I knew we'd reached "email overwhelm" one holiday weekend when my parents were at our home for dinner, and I invited them to stay a little longer. My elderly mom sighed wearily, "Sorry, I guess we'd better go. I need to get home to do email."

Unfortunately, whether employed or retired, most of us are still tapping away. On vacation. At the airport. At the soccer field or gym. At the beach. From a hospital bed—yours or that of a loved one. At bedtime. At sunrise. Over lunch. Chances are, your email habits drain you, both mentally and emotionally. That spells lost productivity for your organization and stress for you. We were told more than two decades ago that email would revolutionize the way we work and save us an enormous amount of time. While email has many benefits, it has also engulfed us and created other productivity drains.

My organization, Booher Research Institute, recently commissioned a survey about email communication habits and productivity from the Social Research Lab at the University of Northern Colorado.[1] Here's what a representative sampling of knowledge workers across multiple industries reported about their email habits (among other things discussed later in this book): Thirty-seven percent spend 1 to 2 hours per day reading and writing email; another 25 percent (one in four workers) spend 3 or 4 hours a day on their email. And, to the question, How often do you *check* email?, 55 percent (more than half) answered that they check email either hourly or multiple times per hour.

Earlier studies confirm our recent research. According to those studies, the average white-collar worker receives 111 to 131 emails per day and spends 2 to 2.5 hours handling incoming and outgoing email. Earlier studies also report hours that people log on during personal time to check work-related email. Some of the studies depended on self-report; others were based on physical sensors, time logs, and email traffic reports.

While some experts predicted back in the 1990s that communication technology could *potentially* improve our productivity by 20–25 percent, a McKinsey Global Institute study found that, in actuality, technology reduces our productivity by 28 percent for any number of reasons—interruptions, distractions, disorganization, and not finding information to reply with.[2]

To calculate the cost to an organization, I'll take a $75,000 salary as an illustration.

White-Collar Worker's Salary at $75,000

1. Multiply the base salary by 1.4 to account for benefits.

   $75,000 (annual salary of employee)

   × 1.4 (salary plus benefits)

   _____

   $105,000 (total annual cost of employee salary & benefits)

2. Multiply total employee cost by percent of time spent on email. Roughly 30 percent of the average worker's time is spent on email, since 2.5 hours/day × 5 days/week = 12.5 hours of a 40-hour week.

   $105,000 (annual employee cost)

   × .30 (percent of time spent on email)

   _____

   $31,500 (total cost to do email 2.5 hrs/day—one employee)

   $315,000 (total cost to do email 2.5 hrs/day—if 10 employees)

   $3,150,000 (total cost to do email 2.5 hrs/day—if 100 employees)

To figure out how much of your own salary you "spend" on email, plug your salary into the above formula. It's easy to see the payoff for learning to tame the email monster and reclaim uninterrupted work time for an employer. The same goes for you, your work success, and your personal life.

WHAT YOU CAN EXPECT FROM THIS BOOK

Besides saving money and time, in the seven chapters of this book, you'll learn how to:

- Identify and stop email clutter—what to stop sending and receiving because it's either counterproductive or harmful to your image
- Compose *better* emails quickly
- Reduce email length so your messages get action
- Organize common-sense files so you can quickly find documents and emails to attach and send
- Avoid security risks and legal liabilities
- Present a professional image when you email clients and colleagues

Today, most substantive correspondence takes place through email. In essence, how you handle email determines the trajectory of your career. Master your emails—make them faster, fewer, and better—and you'll stand out as a clear communicator. And clear communicators become effective leaders in every industry.

So let's get to it. Here are the seven keys to getting through your inbox faster, . . . focusing on the fewer important emails, . . . and writing better emails that build career success.

—*Dianna Booher*

How you handle email determines the trajectory of your career. Master your emails— make them faster, fewer, and better— and you'll stand out as a clear communicator.

CHAPTER 1

Twelve Strategies to Cut the Clutter

> Email is familiar. It's comfortable. It's easy
> to use. But it might just be the biggest killer
> of time and productivity in the office today.
>
> — **RYAN HOLMES,** founder and CEO of Hootsuite

> Email is a system that delivers other people's priorities to
> your attention. It's up to you to decide when that priority
> should be managed into your world. It's not the other way
> around.
>
> — **CHRIS BROGAN,** author, marketing consultant,
>   and social media expert

If you've ever tried to move your belongings into a closet or garage previously used by someone else, you understand this principle: Get rid of all the items that served someone else's purpose before you reload that space. You'll typically sort the previous owner's junk into piles: garbage, donate, sell.

Look at your email box the same way: Over the years, you may have let it become a collection of junk serving everyone's purposes but yours. And your own purposes may have changed over time as your job has changed. So cutting your email clutter can be the easiest way to carve away a big chunk of wasted time.

In the earlier mentioned Booher's University of Northern

Colorado (UNC) survey, a whopping 69 percent of the participants identified clutter as their biggest email problem. More specifically, 34 percent identified "volume" as their number-one email irritant. Other clutter problems included irrelevant emails and redundant emails.

Once you set your mind to the idea of freeing your time, decluttering goes quickly. These twelve basic strategies will help you.

Strategy 1: STOP USING EMAIL FOR TASKS OTHER SOFTWARE HANDLES MORE APPROPRIATELY

When email first came into use, it was the tool of choice for everything: scheduling meetings and appointments, collaborating on projects, reviewing draft documents, and so forth. Today, other software does all these tasks more productively.

Take, for example, the process of scheduling an appointment by email. You can do it the nonproductive way—with five back-and-forth emails:

> John,
> I'd like to discuss this further. How about a call sometime in the next couple of weeks?
> Maria

> Maria,
> Sounds good. I'm traveling Wed–Thurs, but will be in the office Friday. Want to touch base then?
> John

> John,
> What time Friday works for you? I'm available for a call 9–11:00 or 3:00–5:00.
> Maria

> Maria,
> Have a doctor's appointment in the morning. Let's make it 3:00. Which number shall I call?
> John

555-9002

Thanks. Talk soon.

Maria

By contrast, you could use a calendaring software program that would require two actions. Someone sends the calendar appointment request with a suggested time. The recipient either confirms or edits the response to an acceptable appointment time. (Or, if both parties are on the same team and use the same operating system or calendar program, they can just ask the automated assistant to find an empty spot on both calendars and schedule the call.)

Another example of tasks better handled by software other than email is project management. When you're collaborating with coworkers on a team project, obviously you'll be planning, commenting, and giving and receiving feedback and information. According to the UNC survey, fully 62 percent of the respondents still use email more than half of the time to collaborate with their colleagues on projects.

Some of this back-and-forth involving tasks, feedback, and timelines can be handled more easily with project management software rather than email (software like Microsoft Project, Basecamp, Asana, Workzone, or Smartsheet). With such software, your project tasks and related feedback, updates, and images can be added into a "running log" that everyone involved can access and add to, keeping related items and comments all together in one place.

Inappropriate tools clutter and slow your progress.

Strategy 2: STOP USING YOUR INBOX FOR STORAGE

When emails that require action hit their inbox, some people leave them there as reminders of what they need to do—later.

A better plan: If you're using Microsoft's Outlook email, you can simply pull that email over and drop it onto your to-do task pane on the appropriate date for follow-up. Or use the shortcut keys in Outlook to add an item to your tasks. If you're using a different email system, make a manual calendar note—even a note on a paper calendar—of what to do when. Then file the email along with the appropriate contact or project. (See tips in chapter 5, "Organizing Folders and Files.")

Other "storage" clutter results from indecisiveness. Important emails arrive that get attention—but puzzle you because you don't know where best to file them. So they remain in your inbox for days, creating clutter while you decide where to put them for safekeeping. Then, every so often, you have to reread them to remember the pending action and details, wasting time again.

Read your email ONLY once. Think. Decide. Do. Either delete, reply, forward to someone else to handle, or schedule for later action and file it.

Strategy 3: ASK TEAM MEMBERS TO STOP HITTING "REPLY ALL" AND STOP DOING SO YOURSELF

REPLY ALL can clutter your inbox quickly. Instead, send your congratulatory comment directly to the person who deserves the kudos. Offer thanks directly to the person or team who helped you. Turn down the invitation only to the appropriate person. Why clog up seventeen other inboxes, only to have all seventeen of the recipients echo back to you?

A good rule of thumb on the REPLY ALL feature: Is your response helpful to all the others on the distribution list? If not, fly solo. Granted, changing the culture can be difficult. But aim to set the example.

Strategy 4: STOP HANGING ON AND PILING ON WITH MEANINGLESS RESPONSES

You may have caught yourself in the habit of hanging on, wondering where to stop meaningless messages, such as in this back-and-forth series:

Draft report attached.

Ok. Thanks.

You're welcome. Let me know when finished.

Will do. Probably Thursday.

That works.

Maybe sooner.

Fine. No problem.

Enough already! Just stop. Yes, these emails are short. Granted, they don't take much time to write or read. But that's not the point. They clutter. They break your focus. They distract you from more important thinking and doing.

Another clutter practice: "Piling on." Francesca sends out a summary report for the quarter, giving her team a chance to review it before she sends it up the ladder to the executive management team. Seventeen responses flood your inbox: *"Looks good." "Sounds great." "Perfect." "Thanks for this." "Great summary." "Nice job." "Well done." "Nothing to add." "You've covered it!"*

Vince emails the office to say he's sick and not coming in to work. Five emails hit your inbox in the next two hours: *"Sorry you're sick." "Feel better soon." "Got you covered, ole man!" "Hope it's not the flu. Drink, drink, drink—but lay off the hard stuff!" "Thanks for staying home and not exposing the rest of us!"*

Distractions, distractions, distractions as they pop into your inbox. Sure, such emails may build camaraderie—but they can irritate and overwhelm you on a busy day.

Help others break the routine habit of piling on. As the sender, state in your email: *"I'm enclosing the quarterly report for your review before I forward it to the executive team Friday. If you have anything to add or see any corrections to be made, reply to me directly. Otherwise, no reply or action is necessary."*

Strategy 5: ACKNOWLEDGE RECEIPT
AND RESPOND WITH YOUR PLAN

When someone requests action or information from you and you can't act or provide that information right away (because it isn't yet available, it will take an unusually long time to prepare, or you're waiting on someone else to comply), acknowledge the request and let the requester know when you expect to be able to respond fully.

Otherwise, the sender is left wondering if you received the original email. Quite likely, you'll get another reminder. Or worse, you'll get no reminder at all, and they'll assume you took the requested action. Later, you'll both be in for a nasty surprise.

Yes, even in this day of technological miracles, emails still do go astray before reaching the intended reader. They get routed to a junk folder, trash, or never-never-land. Your quick acknowledgment "Got it. Will send after the numbers become available on Sep 20" puts the reader's mind at ease, allows them to plan, and prevents follow-up reminders from them.

(Yes, you *can* send emails with "receipt requested," but I don't recommend it. Many people resent that tactic, thinking you're subtly communicating, "I don't trust you so I'm covering my bases.")

Just as a side note here, an astonishing number of administrative assistants send and respond to emails under their boss's name. Many report that they're allowed to delete emails before their boss even sees them. So it's understandable that people fear you did not actually see an important email and give direction or make a decision about it.

Acknowledging receipt will eliminate a great many reminder and follow-up emails. Just a simple "Got it. Will get back to you shortly" keeps the sender from wondering, Did the email arrive? Can she provide that information before this project is due? Is he or is he not willing to make the referral?

Ask typical *readers* why they don't respond on a timely basis with an answer or information, and they'll likely give one of these reasons for the delay.

- "I didn't know you needed it by (fill in the date)."
- "I didn't know it was urgent."
- "I've been busy on other priorities. I was planning to get to it in the next few days."
- "I've been trying to figure out what you wanted."

As a *writer*, instead of flooding inboxes with reminders and follow-ups and wasting your time to draft them, why not aim to remove the reasons from the outset?

- If you have a deadline for response, state it specifically and clearly.
- Bold print or uppercase the date and place it in a separate paragraph so that it gets attention. If appropriate, add the due date to your subject line.
- Place your request up front, not buried at the end of your email. (See the MADE Format™ on page 27 for the appropriate email structure.)
- If response by a specific date is urgent, say so and explain why in terms of benefits or consequences to the reader. ("... *by Oct 2 so that you'll receive reimbursement within 5 days. If your information is not submitted by that date, reimbursement may be delayed up to 60 days.*")
- Make the necessary response as simple as possible. Can you send a template, form, model, or another resource to help the reader provide the information?
- Include a direct phone number, email address, or link to get more information or help in sending what you want.
- Phrase questions specifically if you expect clear answers. For example, a vague series of questions will likely get a wishy-washy, rambling response—if some are not overlooked altogether.

> Robert,
>
> What are your thoughts about doing a client survey? Other firms have done one simply for marketing purposes, i.e., to let clients know about new service offerings. Some firms survey clients just to identify needs or satisfaction levels. Survey all? Some? Ideas? Michaela

You will get a far better response with a list of specific questions.

> Robert,
>
> We are considering a client survey to identify current satisfaction levels. But there are other reasons, of course, for such surveys, such as introducing services or reminding clients of services we offer. What are your thoughts on the survey idea please?
> — In your mind, what should be the primary goal for our survey?
> — Should we survey all clients or a representative few?
> — Could your team handle this in-house, or should we use a contractor?
> Michaela

Eliminating the above reasons people need reminders and follow-up is not guaranteed to produce results for all the people all the time. But it whittles the number of reasons down to a manageable size.

Strategy 6: CULL YOUR DISTRIBUTION LISTS

Chances are great that you get copied on many emails you don't need. Their usefulness to you has long since passed, but you've found it quicker and easier just to delete those periodic emails than to reply and take yourself off the distribution list permanently. In fact, according to the UNC survey, knowledge workers report that fully 35 percent of the emails they receive are either irrelevant (22 percent) or redundant (13 percent). (Irrelevant emails refer to those about topics that do not apply to the recipient. Redundant emails are those with the same information sent by multiple people.)

That "quick and easy" decision is understandable when you're dealing with just one email. But over time, that decision amounts to hundreds or even thousands of distractions and deletions. So make the best decision for your long-term productivity.

You may be surprised to discover that culling your distribution lists for emails you send may increase engagement with the interested on important projects. As with meetings, the larger the group, the lower the individual participation. When emailing for input, the same principle applies: When you copy a large list, people feel anonymous, and fewer feel it's necessary to respond. If you need their input, cut the list and you'll increase response—not to mention clearing inboxes for the uninterested.

Another drawback of sending emails to people who don't need what you're sending: You're training people to ignore what you send and miss things they really need. Like politicians who spout off about every issue, some emailers earn a reputation for sending useless information.

Strategy 7: STOP RESPONDING ON CC'S SENT FOR PROMOTION OR PRESSURE

Hidden agendas. Backhanded compliments. CYA attempts. Whatever the label, you recognize these tactics when you see them. For example, in emails . . .

- Congratulating team members on a job well done, with copies to a dozen other department heads (sent by the team leader who has accomplished the miracle)

- Thanking the executive team "for their support" on a project that just happens to include a couple of glowing client testimonials about personal contributions to the project's success (high-visibility move?)

> An email cannot be both a productivity tool
> and a weapon. While it may motivate some,
> it will demoralize others.

- Reminding someone about upcoming project deadlines, including details about someone's past delays, with copies to their boss, executive staff, and other department heads (anybody feeling pressure?)

When you respond to such Cc emails about projects and issues not directly involving you, this encourages the sender to keep up the self-promotion and the pressure tactics on colleagues. If you're ever tempted to send such emails yourself, stop. Think.

If you're angry and want to vent, by all means, put that in an email. Just don't send it. Wait. Let it cool off. Overnight is best. But even an hour helps. If the situation is a crisis, then call in an objective colleague to edit out the hot words before you hit SEND. Also, the phone still works as a cooling-off device. Calling the subject of your anger directly removes the mask of anonymity and tends to put you back into a civil frame of mind.

This strategy in particular may demand a new mindset and a major emotional adjustment. An email cannot be both a productivity tool and a weapon. While it may motivate some, it will demoralize others.

Strategy 8: ALLOW PEOPLE TO BOW OUT AFTER INTRODUCTIONS
When someone introduces you to a colleague via email, there's no need to keep the introducer in the loop on the next dozen emails that pass between you and the colleague—unless the introducer wants to stay informed. And if you're the introducer, make it clear to the two colleagues whether you want to be Cc'd on future emails or would like to bow out of their communication:

> Josh and Rita, . . . I'm happy to introduce you
> and hope I've given you enough details here
> about the project—where I think both of you
> could collaborate in a meaningful way. Please
> take it yourselves from here. . . ."

When you get this kind of introduction, then please stop copying the person who introduced you. The introducer wants to get off your copy list and back to his or her own to-dos. If you're the one being introduced, either accept the baton or ask for further clarification:

> Thanks, MacKenzie! Josh and I will put our
> heads together and see if we can come up
> with a plan to beat this deadline. I'm taking you
> off the copy list. But if you want an update at
> any point, let us know.

Strategy 9: STOP FORWARDING JOKES, RANTS, CAUSES, AND ANNOUNCEMENTS

These emails elicit replies—often with questions, to which you then must reply. Before long, you're engaged in a full-fledged discussion.

But far more time-consuming than just one email or discussion is the precedent you've set with the readers who receive your email. You've established the reputation that you have time for and like to receive such cartoons, stories, political commentaries, games, polls, and whine-arounds.

"Announcements by owner" probably get the most attention: New policies. New processes under consideration. New employees. Terminations. New products or services. New marketing campaigns. New research. Financial news. First, there are the rumors. Then the unofficial announcements via the email "back channel" from those who want to be the first to let you know. Then the official announcement by the official person whose job it is to tell you.

Unsubscribe to unwanted emails rather than simply deleting them.

If you're in the back channel, stop pushing your email out into the flow at that point. Decide to let the official "owner of the news" tell the news.

Strategy 10: UNSUBSCRIBE TO E-ZINES YOU NO LONGER NEED

Most senders now have a safe way to unsubscribe. Don't let FOMO (fear of missing out) keep you hanging on someone's list "just in case." After a vacation, or even after a long holiday weekend, it's these extra emails nagging for your attention that push you over the edge. These nonessential promotional emails and newsletters can double or triple those collecting in your box, making you feel as though you can never catch up.

Strategy 11: RE-SORT TO RESPOND AFTER LONG ABSENCES

You probably routinely keep your inbox sorted by date received. But when you return to your inbox after being away for a few days, you may want to re-sort emails by Sender. This sort pulls all the emails by boss Nikki together and by coworker Gregg together.

Here's how this speeds up your responses: Often, people send a first email on topic X. Then they send a second email with a correction on topic X. Then a third email arrives with a new detail about topic X. Then a fourth email asks a question on topic X. If you sort by sender, you can read them all together and send one response, deleting four emails at once.

Strategy 12: TURN OFF EMAIL ALERTS
OR DISABLE AUTOMATIC RETRIEVAL

In the UNC survey, 55 percent of the participants said they keep their email open either *always* (37 percent) or *most of the time* (18 percent). That's a major distraction from your work— unless your primary job is to read and respond to email.

Instead, handle emails only two or three times a day: ideally in the early morning, after lunch, and at the end of the day. Responding every time an email pops into your box breaks your concentration, wasting minutes and energy with each interruption. Productivity studies show there's no such thing as multitasking—just rapid attention-switching, which in itself creates stress, increases the chance for error, and reduces overall efficiency.[3]

■ ■ ■

Okay, you have a dozen strategies to guide your thinking about efficiency and effectiveness. Apply one or several to declutter your email inbox over a couple of weeks. Then adopt the decluttering mindset as you make your way into a brave new world of freedom.

At this point, you may be thinking, "But what about everybody else—all those people who keep practicing bad habits?" You'd be right to be concerned. Changing the culture and habits of others requires leadership. If you're the leader, you can share the strategies and tips in this book and insist that your team members follow them. If you're not in charge, then recommend and set the example.

In either case, you stand to gain time and reduce stress.

CHAPTER 2

Think First to Include the Right Information for the Right People

If it takes a lot of words to say what
you have in mind, give it more thought.

—**DENNIS ROTH,** American diplomat, serving in the
State Department under President George H. W. Bush

"If you want to be a writer, then write." That's the advice successful novelists often give to wannabes. Their point: Stop complaining about the difficulty in finding a literary agent, the rigged best-seller list, the slim chance of getting a contract with a major publisher, the lonely writer's life—and just get down to business. Write! Produce something people want to read.

That's good advice for book authors—but bad advice for email writers.

Doing a brain dump just to capture all your information and ideas in print is rarely a productive habit. When you approach writing an email that way, you'll have to reword almost every sentence in your first draft. After you rearrange ideas into the most logical format, the email rarely flows appropriately. Sentences refer to people, places, dates, or reasons you haven't yet mentioned.

Think
BEFORE
you write.

Give thought to structure before sentences. Drafting your brain dump just to get something on the screen is a time-waster. On the other hand, the second biggest time-waster is staring at a blank screen, trying to decide how to draft the perfect email on the first attempt. Forget these two extremes.

Consider a better way: Think *before* you write.

ANALYZE YOUR AUDIENCE, YOUR MESSAGE, AND THE SITUATION

Consider the following questions in your analysis.

Who Will Read Your Email?

Before you start to write, have the specific name of a reader or groups in mind (example: Supplier Ryan Johnson, your own internal marketing team of three specialists, your boss).

Instead of composing an email about a situation or topic and then deciding who should get a copy, reverse the process. Consider who has interest in the situation: One reader? An entire project team? The entire client organization? If you're writing outside your organization, will your client or vendor likely pass your email on to still other advisors for input, decision, or action?

Assess that audience carefully so that, if practical, one email can handle the entire situation from beginning to end. That is, with the final action in mind, you can email your reader with all the appropriate information so that the primary reader can forward your email to a staffer, delegating the action steps. No further "clarifying" emails from you will be necessary.

For example, can you email client Jeremy that his project is completed and simply copy your finance specialist Lela so she knows to initiate the invoice?

What's of Primary Interest to Your Reader(s)?

Many email writers start with a "once upon a time" perspective. They begin with background information on what *they* are trying to accomplish, what *they* need, and how the reader can help *them* achieve *their* goal. Wrong approach!

Example 1 gives an example of that backward view.

You'll want to take a different approach. What's the key message of interest to these Dallas readers? Probably *not* what Frank's company is doing on the weekend. Instead, they're probably far more interested in how Frank's weekend benefits *them*—the offer of a free pass to the Expo. That offer should be the lead (see example 2).

Why will readers care what you have to say? What do they need to know? What does your message mean for how they will do their job in the next day or month? How can you summarize that message to them in a sentence or two?

Your readers must see immediate relevancy. Don't just identify a *topic* of interest. Your job involves drafting a message or drawing a conclusion about that topic or situation.

Greetings to My Dallas Colleagues:

This coming weekend (April 18–19) my company and I will be participating at the Franchise & Business Opportunities Expo happening at the Dallas Market Hall, 2200 Stemmons Freeway. If you or anyone you know would like to take advantage of a free pass to the event, please respond to this email to let me know. For more details, go to www.DallasFranchiseExpo.com and check things out for yourself.

All the best,
Frank

EXAMPLE 1. An email from the writer's point of view— wrong approach!

Greetings to My Dallas Colleagues:

If you or someone you know would like a complimentary ticket to the Business Opportunities Expo happening at the Dallas Market Hall, 2200 Stemmons Freeway, this weekend (April 18–19), I can send a pass your way. Just email to let me know.

My company and I will be participating in the Expo and would like to see you there. For more details, go to www.DallasFranchiseExpo.com and check things out for yourself.

All the best,
Frank

EXAMPLE 2. Write from your readers' point of view. What are THEY interested in knowing?

What Do Your Readers Already Know?

Try not to tell readers what they already know. This might seem like common sense—but it's not common practice. Writers often spend one, two, three, or even more paragraphs providing background before they get to the point. As a result, readers often stop before they get to the core message, thinking the email is redundant, irrelevant, and/or irritating.

Some examples of telling readers what they already know include:

- Repeating detailed meeting discussions when all recipients attended the meeting
- "Verifying information" when the client/vendor initially provided that same information earlier
- Repeating questions rather than just answering them in a way that makes the referenced questions obvious (*"Last week at the staff meeting you asked me about whether I planned to attend the TRX*

Conference next spring. I've looked at the speakers now, and I don't think that . . ." Better to start your email: *"After reviewing the speakers for the TRX Conference next spring, I don't plan to attend."*)

How Technical or Non-Technical Are Your Readers?

Decide what terms you need to define and how detailed or cursory you should be in providing explanations about such things as testing procedures or cost calculations. If you don't know whether you'll have "pass-on" readers for your email beyond the initial addressee, a good rule of thumb is to summarize in your email and then attach any technical explanations with spreadsheets, graphs, tables, or charts.

How Will Readers Likely React to Your Message?

Will your reader(s) be pleased with your message? Unhappy? Skeptical and argumentative? Is your recommendation or request a low priority for them? Will someone have to lose face to accept what you have to say? Will the readers oppose what you're saying and try to discredit your information or sources?

Consider these various reactions—the good, the bad, and the ugly—and plan what, if anything, you might do to minimize a negative reaction and get a better outcome. For example, if the reader will be skeptical about your conclusion, what can you add to increase credibility?

If the reader will lose face for a past decision because of your new message, how could you phrase your message so that past decisions do not look as though they were foolish at the time they were made? If the reader will tend to consider your request a low priority, what can you include in the email to make the message more urgent?

What's the benefit of responding to your request—or consequence of failing to respond? For example, if they respond within forty-eight hours, will they get their expense reimbursement check within a week? Will their failure to respond to your email mean their name will not be submitted to the list of nominees for the upcoming field trip?

Don't simply hope for the best. Plan for the best.

The typical email starts with a line similar to this: "Hi, Carlos, I hope you're doing well . . ." That's the newest cliché to replace the former opener: "Olivia, I got your March 16 email, in which you asked me several questions about . . ." And that cliché opener replaced this one: "Dear Bradley, This is to acknowledge receipt of your March 16 email, which contained several questions about . . ."

The friendly, less-formal style works well. But any verbatim, often-repeated statement becomes a cliché that simply stands in the reader's way of getting to the point. Granted, a one-sentence cliché opener is not overly bothersome to jump past. But longer, off-topic openings may cause a reader to miss your message altogether. After all, the brief viewing pane for emails provides limited space for readers to make a "read now" or "read later" decision.

To make sure your message gets read, structure your message in the MADE Format™. Then if you'd like to add a friendly sentence or two to build rapport, tack that on at the close.

The MADE Format™ for Emails

The MADE Format™ for organizing emails provides an easy-to-understand structure that helps readers grasp your message quickly.

Remember that you're emailing with a message—not just a topic or a subject. Give your conclusion or point of view about the topic or situation. To distinguish between the two—as well as to solve the problem of staring at a blank screen trying to decide how to start—here's a good trick.

Prime the pump with this opening phrase: "I'm writing to tell you that . . ." and then finish the statement. After finishing the statement, go back and delete "I'm writing to tell you that." What remains will be your opening summary message.

The MADE Format™ for Organizing Emails

M = Message   Summarize your message in one or two sentences.

A = Action   Make recommendations based on your message. Or state any follow-up actions for the reader or next actions you yourself plan to take based on the message.

D = Details   Elaborate on the details as necessary: Why? How? Who? When? Where? How much? For example: Why take the action? How should they take the action? When was the testing done? Where are the changes being made? How much will this cost? How many people/departments will be affected? (Some details can be answered in a single word or phrase. If so, those details will likely be included in the message or in the action statement. But if the details need elaboration, do so here.)

E = Evidence   Mention any optional attachment(s) to make the message or action clearer, easier, or more persuasive. Examples: Cost analysis, contract, map, form, diagram, checklist, invoice, application, org chart.

An easy-to-understand structure helps readers
grasp your point and key details quickly.

If this prompt won't work for you, then you know you don't have a real message. Instead, you have only a topic. Try it:

"I'm writing to tell you that the volatile
stock market this quarter."
*[Not a message; only a topic. What about
the volatile stock market this quarter?]*

"I'm writing to tell you that the volatile stock
market this quarter makes an IPO a risky
decision for us in the short-term."
[A real summary message.]

"I'm writing to tell you that improving
customer satisfaction scores."
*[Not a message; only a topic. What about
improving customer satisfaction scores?]*

"I'm writing to tell you that customer satisfaction
scores have improved by 37 percent during the
past 9 months due to the new return policy."
[A real summary message.]

Think first. Then write.

Now that you've analyzed your audience, know your message, and have a specific action in mind, you're ready to compose or reply to those emails. The hard part—the thinking—is done.

To practice *thinking* in this format, review and compare the "before" and "after" emails in examples 3–8.

You're probably thinking, "Are there any exceptions or variations to this structure?"

Yes, of course. Three:

Transmittals. With a transmittal, the attachment becomes the message. A transmittal email basically says, "I'm sending you something. Here it is." It serves as a place-holder stating what was sent to whom on what date. Generally your transmittal should also summarize the attachment in a sentence or two. For example: *"I'm forwarding the previous Walton contract that contains the clause restricting the option for subcontractors on the project. (See page 8, clause 6.2.)"*

Directives. With a directive, the action becomes the message. Do or don't do this or that.

Bad news. On occasion, even bad-news messages should follow the MADE Format™. But if you are writing outside your organization and have totally different goals from your reader, you may want to soften the bad news by reversing the structure: Start with a neutral or positive statement. Explain the situation, criteria, or your reasoning. Then state the bad news. After the bad news, offer an alternative to meet the person's goals, if possible. Finally, reestablish rapport with a goodwill statement about the future (see example 9).

"Before" Email with Buried Summary and Action

Darren,

The recent function sponsored by Pilboro for our engineering group held at the Aquarium was a tremendous success for us. From previous CRTSA functions we've sponsored, the number of estimated attendees (225–250) was very realistic. The attraction of the Aquarium was most appealing to this group, and therefore a crowd of more than 475 attended.

> *[Great. They were pleased with our service.]*

With the unexpected overflow crowd, I understand the lack of enough food. In that regard, you and your staff handled themselves very nicely.   *[Good. The food issue wasn't a problem.]*

But I'm very disappointed in another matter. When we originally agreed on the Aquarium for this event, the facility was to be exclusively for our organization and its attendees. Needless to say, you did not abide by that agreement. Instead, you held another function in the area where we planned to conduct our entertainment session.   *[Oh. They're still unhappy!]*

You mention stress put on your staff, but I want you to know that this is a significant event for our engineering group and their management team. Your decision to schedule another client group for this same space in the Aquarium put me in a very difficult position. You took space away from us that was part of our original agreement.   *[Very unhappy!]*

In my opinion, the proposal that our representative, Tina Gibbons, presented to you, is fair and forgiving. You and I want this handled professionally and quickly, so please review your numbers once again and take into consideration our position so we can finalize our proposed payment for this event.   *[So that's his point!]*

Sincerely,
Pierre Gustavson

EXAMPLE 3. Don't bury your point at the end of your email.

"After" Email in the MADE Format™

Darren,

We need a resolution on the open contract with your organization regarding the event Pilboro sponsored at the Aquarium on October 5 for our engineering group and management team.   *[Message]*

When we originally agreed on the Aquarium for this event, the facility was to be exclusively for our organization and its attendees. Needless to say, you did not abide by that agreement. Instead, you held another function in the area where we planned to conduct our entertainment session.   *[Message]*

The proposal that our representative, Tina Gibbons, presented to you is fair and forgiving. Please review your numbers once again and take into consideration our position so we can finalize our proposed payment for this event.   *[Action]*

This is a significant event each year for our engineering group and their management team. Your decision to schedule another client group for this same space in the Aquarium put me in a very difficult position. You took space away from us that was part of our original agreement.   *[Detail: Who & Why]*

From previous CRTSA functions we've sponsored, the number of estimated attendees (225–250) was very realistic. The attraction of the Aquarium was most appealing to this group, and therefore a crowd of more than 475 attended. With the unexpected overflow crowd, I understand the lack of enough food. In that regard, you and your staff handled themselves very nicely. But scheduling this extra group in our space is another issue altogether—something strictly forbidden in our contract.   *[Detail: How Many & Why]*

I've reattached our proposed payment. Shall we handle this professionally and quickly? Please contact Tina Gibbons with your response.   *[Attachment & How To]*

Sincerely,
Pierre Gustavson

EXAMPLE 4. Make your message clear from the beginning of the email.

"Before" Email with Buried Summary and Action

Hi, Kirsten—

Because of his connection with you on LinkedIn, James George, Chairman of George Financial Franchises and Catopia, suggested that I share some facts.

[About what?]

James's passive Catopia investment became a major focus, resulting in James becoming, in addition to the founder, also a franchisee and area developer. We talk about this business as having the same timing and explosive growth potential as did his development and sale of Forrestry Financial Real Estate.

[Why are you telling me this?]

This industry is booming, the real estate segment is hot, and we are defining the financial franchise "space" as the leader of the pack. If you are interested in discovering why this investment is so exciting, I have put together some industry highlights. Follow this link for the white paper: CLICK HERE. *[Good for you. Why tell me?]*

Knowing you are a business leader, I've written with the intent to start a conversation and explore if you are interested in multi-unit development as a Catopia franchisee. You can download Catopia franchise specifics HERE. If you would like to discuss this further, please call anytime on my cell at 555-998-1234.

[Oh. I might be. What are the details again?]

Regards,
Madison

EXAMPLE 5. Don't make your readers
have to reread your emails.

"After" Email in the MADE Format™

Hi, Kirsten—

Because of his connection with you on LinkedIn, James George, Chairman of George Financial Franchises and Catopia, suggested that I explore with you setting up a conversation to discuss your interest in a multi-unit development as a Catopia franchisee.

[Hmmm. I'm intrigued.]

If you are interested in discovering why this investment is so exciting, I have put together some industry highlights. Follow this link for the white paper: CLICK HERE. You can download more Catopia franchise specifics HERE.

[Ok. I'll click.]

James's passive Catopia investment became a major focus, resulting in James becoming, in addition to the founder, also a franchisee and area developer. We talk about this business as having the same timing and explosive growth potential as did his development and sale of Forrestry Financial Real Estate.

[Details: Who, Why.]

This industry is booming, the real estate segment is hot, and we are defining the financial franchise "space" as the leader of the pack.

If we've piqued your interest and you'd like to discuss this further, please call anytime on my cell at 555-998-1234 so I can answer more specific questions.   *[Details: How to.]*

Regards,
Madison

EXAMPLE 6. Structure your emails in the MADE Format™ to improve clarity.

"Before" Email with Buried Summary and Action

Brad,

Today, major corporations have realized the importance of improved call center services in meeting their sales and operational goals. Universal, Inc. is very experienced in these applications due to its relationship with Microsoft, Apple, FLEX Power, and First United Resources. These firms, with demanding capacity and survivability requirements like Atlanta TeleServe, have all benefited from our experience in enterprise networking.

[What does this have to do with me?]

Universal, Inc. has been very successful in working closely with its customers to develop a strategy that works best for both the account and its end users. Our CallBest Enhanced Management Applications have provided productivity and performance tools that have assisted both large corporations and emerging institutions as well. I have enclosed literature on CallBest and the Universal R, as well as our efforts on behalf of Microsoft. I hope that you will find these articles of some interest and applicable to your situation.   *[Buried. Why sending?]*

We would like to discuss the potential for future business solutions at Atlanta TeleServe. I am aware of your growth into Tobern as well as your successful operation here in Boise. Before you grow again, please read the Microsoft application; I believe there are applications and expectations that both companies share.

[Oh. Buried action. So that's your point!]

Best,
Kevin

EXAMPLE 7. Readers get lost in this once-upon-a-time format.

"After" Email in the MADE Format™

Brad,

Congratulations on your explosive growth at Atlanta Teleserve into Tobern, as well as your successful operation here
in Boise. I believe your company and ours share the same
expectations and applications (such as CallBest Enhanced
Management and Universal R).   *[Message: New info]*

I'd like to set up a meeting to discuss these potential business
solutions with you after you've had a chance to review the
articles attached here. Later in the week, I'll phone to see
what time might work best for you.

[Action. I might be interested.]

Universal, Inc. has been very successful in working closely
with its customers to develop a strategy that works best for
both the account and its end users. Our CallBest Enhanced
Management Applications have provided productivity and
performance tools that have assisted both large corporations
and emerging institutions as well.

[Details: Why. Who. How.]

Universal, Inc. is very experienced in these applications due
to its relationship with Microsoft, Apple, FLEX Power, and First
United Resources. These firms, with demanding capacity
and survivability requirements like Atlanta TeleServe, have all
benefited from our experience in enterprise networking.

I think you'll find the enclosed literature on CallBest and the
Universal R, as well as our efforts on behalf of Microsoft,
specifically applicable to your situation.

[Good. I'll take a look.]

Best,
Kevin

EXAMPLE 8. Use the MADE Format™
so readers grasp the point all along the way.

Bad-News Message to External Readers: Reversed Structure

Alex,

Having just returned from vacation a couple of days ago to an overloaded inbox, I'm a little slow in responding to your email asking for a referral to Max Caperton as a contractor on their new project.   *[Neutral opener]*

As you might guess, my business relationships are very important to me. So when I refer someone to a friend or client, I like to do it wholeheartedly, being able to comment on that person's character, their excellence in service, and the results I've personally known them to achieve. *[Criteria]* Considering our very short-term relationship of only a few months and very limited interaction, I don't feel comfortable in making a referral to Max at this time.   *[Bad News]*

Have you thought of asking someone else on the team who has worked with you personally? Perhaps they could speak to Max of their personal experience in working with you and give a much more valuable recommendation than I could at this point.   *[Alternative]*

I do wish you the best as you bid on this upcoming contract, and I am looking forward to an opportunity to get to know you better in the future.   *[Goodwill statement]*

Regards,
Stephano

EXAMPLE 9. You may want to present your reasoning/criteria first when your message is bad news. Such a structure tends to "soften the message" while still giving a firm answer.

Writers often ask, "But what about the setup? I shouldn't just jump into the message right off, should I?" In most situations, yes. If you feel the need for a rapport-building statement to begin your email, no harm done—unless you ramble on too long. (Example: Mention a mutual friend, common interest, past connection, or some appreciation.) But often such a statement works just as well, or even better, to close the email and prevents you from having to repeat yourself in a wrap-up line.

Other than these three variations (transmittals, directives, and bad news), you'll do well to use the MADE Format™.

M: The bottom-line summary *message* about an issue

A: Next *actions* you want from the reader (follow-up actions or recommendations) or any actions you plan to take

D: Any necessary *details* that need elaboration (often the why and how need further explanation)

E: Any attachments as *evidence* to clarify, persuade, or make the action easier

REMEMBER THE ONE-MESSAGE, ONE-EMAIL RULE

Invariably, when you try to tackle more than one topic per email, the drafting becomes clunky and, more importantly, your reader will typically pick up on one message and miss the other. Another dilemma for the reader: What to do when one topic in the email needs to be forwarded for action or input and the other message is unrelated and will only confuse the second reader?

Example 10 shows a multi-message email that will likely split the reader's attention.

Hi, Lee—

I'm writing to recap the strategies we discussed and agreed on during our August 22 meeting with the nurse administrators. I believe the following steps are consistent with your guidelines:

Step 1—Pending Orders: We will attempt to standardize all our orders before one nurse administrator for the entire hospital places them with the pharmaceutical companies.

Step 2—Maintenance Reports: Jack will meet with the engineering staff to determine the recurring service problems with the hospital beds and then contact the supplier involved. This information will also be used to develop a service/maintenance program for all hospitals.

Step 3—Task Force Standardization: This task force will be created and charged with determining key features for all surgical beds.

Step 4—Inventory Update: The hospital system will conduct a complete bed assessment to include a replacement program and timeline.

Lee, I hope this recap is consistent with your requests at the meeting. We will proceed accordingly unless we hear differently from you. At our last meeting, we also initiated an effort that could be extremely valuable to Bowen Systems over the long term, namely creating a corporate relationship with all our bed suppliers—not just one. Would you please provide more detail about what you have in mind—how all potential relationships (economic and otherwise) can be enhanced by a "partner contract."

[Buried 2nd message—this likely will be missed.]

I can't thank you enough for your participation and direction with this standardization program. Your vision could create a valuable and innovative tool for the management of inventory, which is easily a $10 million issue for us.

Janelle

EXAMPLE 10. Avoid multiple messages in a single email.

The writer of this email has two summary messages and two actions:

First Message:
I've recapped the guidelines from our meetings.

First Action:
Please confirm that I've understood your guidelines correctly.

Second Message:
I'm also interested in setting up corporate relationships with all our suppliers.

Second Action:
Would you please give me more detail on how to do this—particularly the partner contract?

It's highly likely that the reader, Lee, will focus on (and reply to) one message and ignore the other. Even if Lee decides to provide detail on the partner contract, he may want to forward this email to a staff member to respond and send a boilerplate contract. If so, the opening part of the email will be irrelevant to that second reader.

Filing and later retrieval will also be a problem: Is this about the staff meeting? Or future partnerships? Thus, the general rule: One message, one email. In multi-message emails, one message will inevitably be relegated to play second fiddle.

The general rule:
One message, one email.
In multi-message emails, one message
will inevitably be relegated
to play second fiddle.

USE CC AND BCC PROPERLY

Use the Cc feature when you want your primary reader (and others on the copy list) to see all who've received a copy of the same email. That alleviates duplication—their forwarding copies to each other.

If the primary reader wants to ask a question of someone on the copy list or delegate a task to them related to the email, that primary reader doesn't need to repeat all the same details. They can just forward your email with their comment or question on top of your previous email.

The Bcc (blind copy) feature may prove more sensitive: With the Bcc feature, your primary reader doesn't know that you've sent a copy to the person listed as Bcc. (The reason for a Bcc might be political—or completely harmless. That is, you may be writing to a client about a meeting cancellation and Bcc someone internally, for example, so they know to cancel related travel arrangements).

Most often, however, the Bcc feature is used when you're sending a blast to a large group and you don't want to reveal everyone's email address—for two reasons, privacy and clutter. If you intend to copy others without having someone hit REPLY ALL, which reveals the addresses of everyone on your list (either intentionally or accidentally), send the email to yourself. Then place all the readers on your Bcc distribution list.

■ ■ ■

With these essentials in mind, you'll write shorter, clearer emails in half the time!

CHAPTER 3

Draft Fast to Be Productive

If you bring that sentence in for a fitting,
I can have it shortened by Wednesday.

—**HAWKEYE**, a character in the American
TV series M*A*S*H, "The Gun"

t this point, you've done the hard part. You've identified all the essentials for even a complex email. Next step: Quickly convert these essentials to complete sentences on the screen. Occasionally, even when you've done your thinking first (while stuck in traffic, eating breakfast, or sitting in a boring meeting), you stare at the keyboard and the exact words won't flow. When that's the case, perfection is the enemy of good. You just need to start first and perfect later.

PRIME THE PUMP TO GET STARTED FAST

Try the trick mentioned in chapter 2 to help you distinguish between a topic and a message. To get a quick start drafting, prime the pump with, *"I'm writing to tell you that . . . ,"* and finish the statement.

Then keep moving along with the action you want from your reader (recommendations or follow-up actions): *"Would you . . ."* Or: *"So I recommend that . . ."* Or: *"That being the case, we are asking that you . . ."* Or: *"Please help us by . . ."*

USE SMOOTH TRANSITIONS SO THE EMAIL FLOWS FAST

If you find yourself stalled as you draft, that difficulty generally happens in deciding how to link the four parts of the MADE

41

Format™. More specifically, after you draft great message and action statements, getting into the details may feel awkward.

Don't let that slow you down. Simply add a good transition statement and then circle back to elaborate or clarify.

> ### Examples of Transition Statements
> "*Let me provide a little background on this situation . . .*"
> "*To elaborate on the reason for this unusual request,
>   our team . . .*"
> "*Let me explain further exactly how this situation
>   developed . . .*"
> "*If you recall, a couple of months ago . . .*"
> "*Let me circle back and fill in a few more details here . . .*"
> "*Note that this new process represents a marked change
>   in our approach . . .*"
> "*Let me explain why the change . . .*"
> "*To help you calculate the projected costs in your area,
>   let me give you an example of how . . .*"

You may be asking, "Why not provide the background and details *first*—before you summarize the message and action?" Good question.

Simple answer: Clarity and speed.

First, clarity. Imagine reading a news story without a headline or lead paragraph. You're just left to wade through all the contradictory quotes, details, and statistics the reporter presents. You'd probably go back and reread the article to see if you could determine what all these details, facts, and stats "mean." In any case, you'd be "in the dark" about the point until well into the article. And certainly, at the beginning, most readers would feel as though the journalist were pulling them into a busy freeway blindfolded.

The same feeling occurs when reading emails structured with "details" first (see example 11). Readers will rarely understand your background information until they have your overview. Having a summary first makes the details clear.

A second reason for the MADE structure: Speed. Once you've drafted the summary message and action statements, you have a roadmap in place. You simply push the details along the cleared path (see example 12).

POLISH YOUR SUBJECT LINES: SPECIFIC, USEFUL, BRIEF

You'll find it quicker and easier to add your subject line *after* you've drafted your email—not before. Why? Because the subject line should be a condensed version of your message and action statements. Subject lines should be informative, not mysterious, unless you're an email marketer. And even then, marketers often find that vague headlines don't always intrigue buyers.

A quick scan of a week's inbox reveals subject lines like these:

> *A Quick Question* (About what?)
> *The Upcoming Denver Workshop* (So what about it?)
> *CRD Coding* (Are you sending or asking?)
> *Are You Available Friday at 1:00?* (It depends.)
> *Following Up* (On what?)
> *Last-Minute Details* (Is the writer asking for them or
>   giving them?)
> *Oops, One More Thing* (What's the "thing"?)

Can you imagine reading newspaper headlines as vague as these: "*War.*" "*Terrorist Attack.*" "*Taxes.*" "*Blizzard Conditions.*" You wouldn't know where to begin reading. Unless you're a novelist—a mystery writer at that!—turn your subject lines into informative headlines.

SUB headlines are **S**pecific, **U**seful, **B**rief.

> *How to Register Family Members for RW Event*
> *May 12–13 Denver Workshop: Cancelled Due to*
>   *Low Enrollment*
> *Stop Work on CRD Coding: Glitch in Step 5*

Email with a Buried Message and Action and No Transition

Dean,

This email is to follow up on our earlier meeting this year. Back in January, we talked in general about potential interest in a blanket purchase order between your organization and Universal.

In January, we responded to your bid #P-2683 for 800 mowers. We proposed both the Bladera and the BladeSpade series. To date, no information from our sealed bid regarding its status has been mentioned. So we're assuming no decision has been made.

I think it's appropriate that we extend an invitation to you and your team members on the committee to visit and tour our Jackson, Mississippi, plant and headquarters. The purpose of this trip would be to focus on specific features in our mower line so we can get accurate information on what your requirements will be going forward.

Currently, we have in place a very informative customer visitation program. I would host the trip and fly with you on our company plane. Our plane can accommodate up to six of your team members, plus me and our crew.

Typically, we would depart Chicago O'Hare at 8:00 a.m. and arrive in Jackson in time for lunch. Afterward, you can see how our product is manufactured and then stop by our product systems center. Accommodations can be made for us at the nearby resort, where dinner and breakfast would be prepared for us. We then could revisit the product systems center before lunch and a 1:00 p.m. departure. We would be back in Chicago later that same afternoon. After this two-day investment, I am sure that 95 percent of your technical questions regarding the equipment will have been answered.

Dean, I would be delighted to hear your thoughts about such a trip. I know we can clear up many questions about which model does what.

Thank you again for your interest in Universal products.

Best regards,
Louis

EXAMPLE 11. Without an overview and clear transitions throughout, readers often waste time in reading details they have no interest in knowing.

Email in the MADE Format™ with Smooth Transitions

Dean,

To help you make a decision about our bid #P-2683 for 800 mowers, we would like to invite you and your team members on the committee to visit and tour our Jackson, Mississippi, plant and headquarters. The purpose of this trip would be to focus on specific features in our mower line (specifically the Blader and the BladeSpade series proposed) so we can get accurate information on what your requirements will be going forward.   *[Message]*

Would you be interested in such a visit? If so, let me know, and I'll make the arrangements immediately.   *[Action]*

Let me outline the trip details here: *[Transition to details]*

I would host the trip and fly with you on our company plane. Our plane can accommodate up to six of your team members, plus me and our crew.   *[Details begin]*

Typically, we would depart Chicago O'Hare at 8:00 a.m. and arrive in Jackson in time for lunch. Afterward, we can see how our product is manufactured and then stop by our product systems center.

Accommodations can be made for us at the nearby resort, where dinner and breakfast would be prepared for us. We then could re-visit the product systems center before lunch and a 1:00 p.m. departure. We would be back in Chicago later that same afternoon. After this two-day investment, I am sure that 95 percent of your technical questions regarding the equipment will have been addressed.

Dean, we have a very informative customer visitation program. So I feel certain that we can clear up many questions about which model does what.

Your thoughts about such a visit?

Best regards,
Louis

EXAMPLE 12. An overview and transitions set the direction that allows quick drafting as well as fast reading.

*Available Friday at 1:00 for Call About Licensing
    Extension?*
Following Up on Your Decision About Menro Investment
*Providing Last-Minute Details on Phone Switchover
    Saturday*
Requesting Approval for $5K Increase in IT Budget for Q3

PAY ATTENTION TO THE PROPER GREETINGS AND SIGN-OFFS

As you draft, don't let deciding on the proper greeting and sign-off stump you and waste your time.

In the classic movie *Jerry Maguire*, Tom Cruise barges into his home after an argument and long separation from his wife, starts an explanation meant as an apology, and makes a romantic plea: "You complete me . . . You . . ."

She interrupts, "You had me at hello."

In case you don't recall the movie plot, let me just say the similarity to email greetings stops there: Your email readers are not in love with you. (Okay, maybe your family members love you.) Even if emailing best friends, chances are they already have an overflowing inbox and may not want another email from you.

So your email greetings should warm readers up—not put them off.

Don't Skip the Greeting

First, assume you need a greeting. Even if you email the same person every day, you never know when a specific email may eventually turn into a long email thread—one that someone else may need to search through later. With no greetings, after an email string gets cold, it's often difficult to determine who said what to whom (unless you always attach your signature block). A greeting on each exchange makes that very clear.

Your email greetings should warm readers up—
not put them off.

Stand Out by "Mixing It Up"

My colleague Bill Lampton has mastered this principle well. Every email from him sounds as though he has just walked into my office with a fresh comment of the morning. Here are some recent greetings from his emails:

> *Dianna, hi—*
> *Very good, Dianna. The next thing we need to . . .*
> *How about Tuesday, Dianna?*
> *Good morning, Dianna!*
> *For sure, Dianna . . . Mid- to late-May fits my schedule . . .*
> *I totally agree, Dianna . . .*

See how these greetings pull you right into the email? Yet to any skimming reader of a long thread, it's still quickly clear who's writing to whom.

Personalize When Possible—Even to a Group

Depending on which email system you use and how clean your list is, you may be able to personalize with individual names. But when you can't, for whatever reason, at least use a personalized group greeting. Examples:

> *Hi, Region 4 Sales Team—*
> *To My Fellow Hurricane Volunteers:*
> *Greetings to Our Loyal Club Members!*

Match the Relationship, Content, and Tone

You'd never walk into a coworker's office laughing, passing along a funny story, and then suddenly say, "And oh, by the way, Michael, I just came from a meeting with the boss. They're going to fire you tomorrow." That would be a jarring switch in content and tone—no matter how close your relationship.

The same is true when communicating by email. Your greeting should match the rest of your email in content, relationship, and tone. If the content is serious, the greeting

should be more formal. If the topic is light and the relationship close, your greeting can be as informal as you'd be face
to face or on the phone. If you're emailing your project team
about cancelling a meeting, your greeting will be informal and
conversational:

> My apologies, everyone . . .
>
> Hi—
>
> Team, A quick update:

If you're threatening a lawsuit against a vendor for non-
performance, your greeting will be formal:

> Ms. Molinas:
>
> I'm disappointed that we've been unable to reach
> agreement in the Ridgeway Bridge matter. That leaves
> us no alternative but to pursue all legal channels to . . .

Punctuate Greetings and Sign-Offs Correctly

An egregious punctuation error at the beginning of an email
flashes "careless writer, unimportant message."

Punctuated like this, these greetings are never correct:

Dear Raul;
Tom;
Good morning Marita,
Hi Gregg

Here are the correct versions:

Dear Raul,   or   *Dear Raul:*
Tom,   or   *Tom—*
Good morning, Marita—   or   *Good morning, Marita,*
Hi, Gregg—   or   *Hi, Gregg,*

Don't let your punctuation be a put-off from the get-go.
Master the proper marks to set the tone and relationship you
intend.

Drop Meaningless Sign-Offs

If the topic is routine and the relationship cordial, avoid ending each back-and-forth response with "Thanks" or "If you have any questions, please don't hesitate to call."

Of course, if these phrases or questions are meaningful to your message, include them. But these comments quickly become clichés. Once you're "into a conversation" simply continue. Just add your name or signature block for ease in skimming a long thread later and following who said what to whom.

TAKE CARE NOT TO BE *TOO* BRIEF

Yes, we've been talking about all the tidbits that help you to draft quickly. And yes, you *can* compose most emails in minutes, if not seconds. But that's not *always* a good thing.

Far too many poor decisions rest on knee-jerk email responses: A boss or team leader emails the project team to ask for input on a dilemma. On his way out the door for a meeting, the first reader replies with a half-baked idea, hitting REPLY ALL.

In turn, other team members all pressed for time working on other projects at the moment, reply with "Fine by me." "Sounds good." "Works for me." "I'm okay with that." And before you know it, the inclination for speed overruns the need for quality thinking.

Don't let fast emails become the enemy of good decisions.

After buying into that quality-thinking principle, feel free to pick up speed.

Just remember that brevity *can* lead to brusqueness—particularly when discussing a sensitive or negative situation or when you haven't yet established a cordial relationship with the reader.

For example, let's say your department is hosting a farewell party for Raymond before he leaves the organization at the end of the week. Party planner Cara wants to make sure she has enough food, so she emails you and several other team members to ask, "Are you going to Raymond's party this afternoon at 3:00?"

You respond, "No."

You may be busy and consider your email simply "to the point." Cara and others interpret that cryptic message negatively: "Do you dislike Raymond?" "Have you had a recent conflict?" "Are you angry with someone else attending?" "Do you not feel part of the group?" "Feeling overwhelmed in your job?" "Depressed? Not in the mood to party?" "Problems at home?"

Adding just one other word or phrase can totally change the tone of a brief email: For example, in the previous situation: "No, sorry I can't make it." Or: "No, must leave early today." "Swamped. Can't attend." "Hardly know Raymond. Busy on a high-priority project today. You guys have fun!"

When drafting quickly, never sacrifice good decision-making, clarity, or tone to be brief.

Far too many poor decisions
rest on knee-jerk email responses.
Don't let fast emails become
the enemy of good decisions.

MAKE THE SIGNATURE BLOCK WORK FOR YOU

As with subject lines, keep your signature block informative, useful, and brief. Those three concepts can't necessarily be translated into a certain number of lines. Some organizational addresses may require six lines while others require only two.

> **Informative.** Recipients need essential contact information—typically your title, organization, address, and phone numbers. The arrangement of items, font size, images, and use of color also affect readability and the total display.

Useful. Sales and marketing people—and others concerned about building their brand—may want to use their signature block to add a tagline helpful to their career. Examples: A new product or service offering, a trademarked slogan, an award, an upcoming industry event or date.

Brief. Lengthy signature blocks annoy readers when they try to skim through long threads. (On most email messages, you can create or attach a shorter email signature on response emails or internal emails to your team.)

Beware the trend of attaching images (such as an image signature, logo, or motivational quotation) to signature blocks. Internet experts peg this practice of including extraneous images as a key reason for email being routed to spam and junk folders.

But once you have a standardized block that fits your emails 99 percent of the time, you've set up a grab-and-go time-saver.

■ ■ ■

At this point, you've drafted a quick email. But don't waste your previous effort by becoming trigger-happy before your final step: editing for clarity, conciseness, grammar, and style.

If your email is an important one, allow a cooling-off period. Overnight is best; an hour will do. Leave it in your draft folder and come back to it with fresh eyes for the editing step.

Not all emails can cost someone their job. But some do. Take one last look.

CHAPTER 4

Edit Last for Clarity, Conciseness, Grammar, and Style

Brevity is a great charm of eloquence.

—**CICERO**, orator, philosopher, and author in ancient Rome

Fact: Every day, 2.67 million apostrophes are brutally, incorrectly forced to make words plural.

—**ANONYMOUS**

If you're writing a one-sentence email, this editing step may take only five to ten seconds. But it's an important step nonetheless.

In the UNC survey, 89 percent of the respondents reported that a poorly written email (improper grammar, poor structure, unclear message or action) lessened the credibility of the sender and the sender's organization. A full 25 percent said that such an email would cause them to reconsider their decision to work with that sender or buy from that person's organization.

But even more important than credibility and image, clarity is at stake. One small blooper (like a misplaced word, a vague pronoun, or a misused comma) can totally change the meaning of your email.

In fact, I estimate that every day, 1.79 bazillion innocent people are charged with misdeeds and crimes they did not commit—such as this one: *"Charles joins our company from Universal. In his spare time, Charles loves hiking, barbecuing his family and antique cars."* (But chances are that Charles is *not* a psycho killer! Somebody somewhere has accused him falsely with this email. He probably does not barbecue his family! Instead, the writer has simply omitted an important comma.)

Okay, let's get serious: The editing step proves essential if you're writing a long email on a technical, controversial, or sensitive subject. Ramble on and you may lose your readers in the details. Fail to emphasize the right phrase in your sentence, and you may fail to persuade. Choose the wrong word and you could create an offense that spurs a lawsuit.

EDIT FOR CLARITY

Remember: Your emails are always clear to YOU—or you wouldn't have written them as you did. Making them clear in the mind of the READER is what counts.

Pay Attention to Eye Appeal

In emails of more than three or four paragraphs, consider whether headings would help your reader preview or locate information quickly. How about a list rather than a paragraph? Keep in mind that a numbered list typically implies an order (such as sequential steps), whereas a bulleted list does not.

Unless there's a good reason not to, break paragraphs after three to five sentences. With a good transition, your reader will follow you into the next paragraph. Don't go to the other extreme, however, writing a series of one-sentence paragraphs. Such choppy emails look disjointed.

Your emails are always clear to YOU—
or you wouldn't have written them as you did.
Making them clear in the mind of the
READER is what counts!

Don't Let Sentences Ramble

Readers don't slog through their emails for entertainment. They want information without having to work for it. When a sentence runs more than two lines (fifteen to twenty words maximum), find the appropriate spot to end it.

> **Too Long:** *The IOD will clear the CG Pointer, run the RAM test, and report the results, then read the app code into IOD RAM using TMA, and a count of the buffers is maintained in the CP flag.*

> **Improved:** *The IOD will clear the CG Pointer, run the RAM test, and report the results. Then the system will read the app code into IOD RAM, using TMA. A count of the buffers is maintained in the CP flag.*

There's tremendous power in words—if you don't link too many of them in a single sentence, especially in a technical sentence like the one above.

Clarify References for *This*, *That*, *They*, *It*, or *Which*

A pronoun refers to a previous noun (person, place, thing, or idea). Just make sure there's only one such logical reference in the context.

> **Vague Reference:** *In this installation, there is only one possible connection, which creates a problem.*
> > [Is the connection itself creating the problem? Or is having only one connection the problem? Note: Technically, *which* must refer to a specific noun— not an idea or the sentence as a whole. But many writers use *which* carelessly to do so, frequently causing misreading. Whatever follows *which* **adds** information about the noun, while *that* **limits** the meaning of the noun it refers to in the sentence.]

Clear: *In this installation, there is only one possible connection that is creating a problem.*

OR:

Having only one possible connection creates a problem.

Vague Reference: *The sponsors provide guidelines to all the various committees. Committees will organize their own task forces to deal with departmental differences. They set up the frameworks, deadlines, and budgets.*
[Who is "they"? Sponsors, committees, or task forces?]

Clear: *The sponsors provide guidelines to all the various committees. Committees will organize their own task forces to deal with departmental differences. The **committees** will also set up the frameworks, deadlines, and budgets.*

Emphasize the Right Idea

In an email, you have several ways to emphasize the most important idea:

- Place the information in the subject line.
- Include the information up front as part of your message.
- Include the information in a heading.
- Bold, underline, or uppercase the word or phrase.
- Use a climactic sentence.

Quite simply, a climactic sentence (also called a periodic sentence) is one that builds to a climax. That is, the most important information or idea goes at the end. The next most important information or idea goes at the beginning. The unimportant clause or phrase stays in the middle. With the following examples, you can see how the writer controls emphasis and what ideas readers are likely to "pick up on"—particularly when they read quickly.

Placement of information in a sentence is to writing what voice inflection is to speech.

Climactic Sentences

Because Ben plans to be traveling frequently in the coming month, he has arranged to pay our year-end bonuses six weeks early.

> [Emphasizes the early bonus, not the travel]

Ben has arranged to pay our year-end bonuses six weeks early because he plans to be traveling frequently in the coming month.

> [Emphasizes the travel, not the early bonuses]

The VP has not yet authorized any bonuses, a fact you may be aware of, but Ben wants to make sure all funds due us are in our hands before the holidays.

> [Emphasizes getting the funds before the holidays. Secondary emphasis: The VP has not authorized the bonuses. Unimportant: You may be aware that the VP hasn't yet authorized the bonuses.]

Ben wants to make sure all year-end bonuses due us are in our hands before the holidays. Do keep in mind, however, that the VP has not yet authorized any bonuses.

> [Emphasizes that the bonuses are not a sure thing yet.]

If you found the previous explanations and illustrations complex, here's why: They're complex only because you're the reader, not the writer. And that's the problem with email. (Stay with me here.) As the *writer* of an email, you understand the situation. As you write, you're probably hearing yourself pronounce the words, *adding the voice inflection in your mind.* So if you omit the punctuation, no big deal. You know what you mean. You're inflecting and pausing to give the words emphasis and meaning.

But the email *readers* enter the situation cold. Recipients have no one reading the email aloud to them, inflecting and pausing in the correct spots. So if the writer omits the correct punctuation or places the words in the wrong spot so that they fail to get the right emphasis, readers may miss the point.

Placement of information in a sentence
is to writing what voice inflection
is to speech.

Change the Subject Line in Long Threads

As long as you're on the same topic, keeping the same subject line on your email thread makes sense. But often the first topic spawns a new subject, and, before you know it, that new topic diverges into a third topic. Eleven responses later, someone notices that the original subject line has absolutely nothing to do with the later discussion.

This "sprawling" discussion in one thread presents a problem for several reasons:

- Difficulty in relocating an email or a single piece of information saved in your database because the subject line doesn't match the topics discussed there

- Confusion created when new readers are copied on subsequent emails with an unrelated subject line

- Unrelated, confusing information created when trying to delegate and/or forward only certain parts of the thread

- Confidentiality issues when a thread is forwarded to new readers (without regard for the original commenters)

So when the topic changes, revise the subject line accordingly. And when the topic of the thread changes substantially, start a new email with a more appropriate subject line.

Make Sure Abbreviations Are Understood

Abbreviations in email do not always serve the same purpose as abbreviations in technical documents. Granted, in both situations abbreviations provide a shortcut for expressing a concept. But among emailers, sharing the abbreviations is about sharing the community and the culture. LOL (laughing out loud), K (ok), FWIW (for what it's worth), IMHO (in my humble opinion), FOMO (fear of missing out) may make your readers feel like insiders. That can be a good thing for the camaraderie it builds.

But when emailing on technical topics, abbreviations can make secondary readers feel like outsiders—totally puzzled and annoyed. Know your audience. Define unfamiliar terms.

EDIT FOR CONCISENESS

The shorter your emails, the less time it takes to write them and read them. Consider these two messages:

Version 1: *The applicant we interviewed yesterday is totally unsuitable for the job.*

Version 2: *The applicant I mentioned to you yesterday whom I'd hope could fill the position was disappointing. In fact, after the interview, my team compared notes and decided that he was totally unsuitable for the job for several reasons that we can go into if you're interested. Let me know if you want to discuss further or would like to explore the possibility of using him elsewhere, but I'm sure this is the least of your concerns now with so many other pressing deadlines.*

If you think Version 1 is the stronger message, I'm with you. The more words you pour into an email, the greater the chance to weaken your message.

Don't write this: *All confidential records that are not explicitly requested by the various department managers will be retained in our confidential files until we receive a written request from a department manager for the necessary file to be sent.*

Write this instead: *We send confidential records only when managers request them in writing.*

Conciseness increases speed and often improves clarity.

Use Strong Verbs

Collapse Clauses and Kill "To Be" Verbs

Replace "to be" verbs in sentences beginning with *there is/are/was/were* or *it is/it was*. Clauses beginning with *who, which,* or *that* can often be folded into the bigger idea.

Weak: *There are several problems to solve on that project before we can notify the client.* [15 words]
Strong: *We need to solve several problems on that project before notifying the client.* [13 words]

Weak: *Sheila Fitzgerald is a Boise client who is always insistent about a 7-day delivery date.* [16 words]
Strong: *Boise client Sheila Fitzgerald always insists on a 7-day delivery date.* [12 words]

Change Passive Voice to Active Voice

In active-voice constructions, the subject does the action of the sentence. In passive-voice constructions, the subject does nothing; it simply receives the action. That is, something happens to the subject.

Passive: *Their financials have been audited twice this year by headquarters.* [10 words]
Active: *Headquarters audited their financials twice this year.* [7 words]

Passive: *The report was submitted to the marketing manager by Jay Sucone.* [11 words]
Active: *Jay Sucone submitted the report to the marketing manager.* [9 words]

Passive: *It is recommended that Universal terminate the contract.* [8 words]
Active: *Universal should terminate the contract.* [5 words]

Passive: *Jaime has already been registered for that training by his manager more than a month ago.* [16 words]
Active: *The manager registered Jaime for that training more than a month ago.* [12 words]

What's the big deal—12 words versus 16 words? Nothing, if you're writing only one sentence. But if you're increasing *every* sentence by 15–25 percent, then the *total* email grows by 15–25 percent. And that increase adds to reading time for everyone on your distribution list!

Cut Little-Word Clutter

Nouns and verbs serve as the sentence skeleton. They carry the "muscle" of your message. They sound factual and authoritative (although they may be wrong). Adjectives and adverbs add the fat. These opinion words add the emphasis, loopholes, and trapdoors. Examples:

This experience proves beneficial only in the case when we bid on things like the Tyson project.
This experience proves beneficial only with bids like the Tyson project.

Our regional director is the type of woman who doesn't take no for an answer.
Our regional director doesn't take no for an answer.

Cut the clutter.

Shelby resigned for a number of factors, including subpar pay, a hostile culture, her micromanaging boss, and a demanding clientele.
Shelby resigned because of subpar pay, a hostile culture, her micromanaging boss, and a demanding clientele.

Our committee talked in terms of deadlines and budgets.
Our committee talked about deadlines and budgets.

The attached template is for your use in preparing that report.
The attached template is for preparing that report.

Eliminate Redundancies
Redundancies come in many forms.

Redundant Nouns: the reason is because, the reason is why, ways and means, separate and distinct, subject matter, goals and objectives, period of time, red in color, at this point in time, large in size, oblong in shape,

a distance of 36 miles, 500 words in length, few
in number, the sum of $600, during the month
of May, summer months, first and foremost

Redundant Ideas: any and all, as a general rule, basic
fundamentals, alternate choices, important essentials,
serious crisis, necessary requisite, close together,
end result, current status, final outcome, future
plans, free gift, past experience, past history, new
breakthrough, close proximity, joint partnership,
conclusive proof, true facts, honest truth, advance
warning, disappear from sight, following after,
foreign imports, equally as well, in two equal halves,
symptoms indicative of, completely surrounded, as
you may or may not know, this particular instance,
exactly alike, precisely correct, null and void,
continue on, grouped together, joined together, refer
back to, try out, plan ahead, repeat again, finish up,
open up, cancel out, circulate around, distribute
around, continue to remain, still persist

Redundancy in your email can be a distraction. That
said, some repetition serves a valid purpose: Emphasis. For
example:

Bidding on this job was a waste of time and money.
Bidding on this job was a total waste of time and
money.   [Adds emphasis]

Have you noticed a decline in Desiree's performance
this past quarter?
Have you yourself noticed a decline in Desiree's
performance this past quarter?   [Adds emphasis]

Pull all these editing-for-conciseness principles together
and you can cut many emails by 30 percent or more (as in
examples 13–14), plus improve readability.

To Our Supporters,

On behalf of 7Secrets, it is my privilege to thank you for your legacy of generosity over the years. Your donations have greatly helped us transform our community! We are a beacon of light and love, with the intent of transforming lives, homes, and our community. In the last five years, we have built 49 homes, provided school supplies for 88,720 children, fed and clothed 317,117 individuals through our Care Center, rallied volunteers to give over 300,000 hours and invested over $12,000,000 into our local community. You are a tremendous blessing and we hope you continue your impact with us this Bromwell Charities Day, October 15!

Thank you!   *(111 words)*

EXAMPLE 13. Wordiness dilutes your impact.

To Our Supporters,

Just a quick thank you for your generosity in helping 7Secrets transform our community! In the last 5 years, together we have built 49 homes, provided school supplies for 88,720 kids, and fed and clothed more than 317,000 people! It adds up to more than $12 million invested in this community. You are a blessing! Hoping we can count on you again on Bromwell Charities Day, October 15.

Thank you!   *(71 words, a 36 percent reduction)*

EXAMPLE 14. Brevity increases impact.

Conciseness increases speed
and often improves clarity.

Consider cutting the clutter to be more like working a hidden word puzzle, where nonsensical letters are arranged in vertical and horizontal rows across the page and your task is to identify and circle the words hidden in the maze. Eliminating the wordiness in your emails takes a few extra seconds or minutes. But your investment pays off for everyone in the communication process.

EDIT FOR GRAMMAR

Proper grammar leads to clarity. Grammar rules provide an aid, not an impediment, to writing—in much the same way that driving "rules" help us navigate safely and prevent traffic accidents.

Avoid Run-on Sentences

The term "run-on sentence" refers to two separate ideas jammed together without proper punctuation—as if they were one thought.

> **Run-On:** *That deadline works for me I'll see you when you return from vacation.*
> **Correct:** *That deadline works for me. I'll see you when you return from vacation.*
> OR:
> *That deadline works for me; I'll see you when you return from vacation.*

> **Run-On:** *Kari's position was eliminated in June, however, she came back to work for us in the same position as a contractor in July.*
> **Correct:** *Kari's position was eliminated in June. However, she came back to work for us in the same position as a contractor in July.*
> OR:
> *Kari's position was eliminated in June; however, she came back to work for us in the same position as a contractor in July.*

Put Descriptors in Their Place

Descriptive words and phrases need to be as close as possible to the noun or pronoun they describe. Otherwise, they can confuse and amuse your reader.

Misplaced Descriptor: *Placing a tarp over the paper goods, the truck was left in the parking lot overnight.*
[Did the truck place the tarp over the paper goods?]
Correct: *Placing a tarp over the paper goods, the workers left the truck in the parking lot overnight.*

Misplaced Descriptor: *Bob told us in June the new offices would be ready for move-in.* [Did Bob tell them in June? Or will the new offices be ready in June?]
Correct: *In June, Bob told us the new offices would be ready for move-in.*
OR:
Bob told us the new offices would be ready for move-in in June.

Use Fragments Only Intentionally

Incomplete sentences (fragments) serve us well in email: *"Got it." "Will respond in full by Monday." "No." "Your thoughts please?" "Can do!"*

The grammatical error that damages your reputation is leaving a fragment when you obviously intended to write a sentence. Usually, the scrap of a sentence becomes a fragment because it has no verb.

Unintended Fragment: *The Denver division, which scheduled a first-of-its-kind driving test to educate consumers on the issues.* [What about that division?]
Complete Sentence: *The Denver division, which scheduled a first-of-its-kind driving test to educate consumers on the issues, has been recognized nationally.*
OR:
The Denver division scheduled a first-of-its-kind driving test to educate consumers on the issues.

Unintended Fragment: *The owner of the sports team, known to many as the most supportive of anyone in the organization.* [What about the owner?]

Complete Sentence: *The owner of the sports team, known to many as the most supportive of anyone in the organization, did not attend.*

OR:

The owner of the sports team is known to many as the most supportive of anyone in the organization.

Make Parallel Ideas Match

If you're writing emails for easy skimming, you'll use frequent lists. That means items in your lists (also in your sentences) need to be parallel—stated in a matching structure. For example, they should all be either phrases or complete sentences. They should all start with a verb, or they should all start with a noun. Any such pattern works—as long as the items in the list match.

Unparallel List: *Feel free to download this white paper on all your devices. We will discuss related topics such as these:*

- *Smartphones, tablets, laptop peripherals*
- *What metrics will engineering students use in the future?*
- *Financial gains and benefits you'll have as members*
- *The university's legal liabilities*

Parallel List: *Feel free to download this white paper on all your devices. We will discuss related topics such as these:*

- *Smartphones, tablets, laptop peripherals*
- *Metrics for engineering students*
- *Financial gains and benefits*
- *Legal liabilities for the university*

Parallelism also matters in sentences. Mismatched ideas lead to misreading, as in this sentence:

Unparallel: *To be considered as a test site, a field office needs proper equipment, to stabilize their output, and they need to have a completed application on file.*

[How many criteria are mentioned here? Two? Three?]

Parallel: *To be considered as a test site, a field office needs proper equipment, stable output, and a completed application on file.*

[All items match.]

Make Subjects and Verbs Agree

Both the subject and verb should agree in number—either singular or plural. Mistakes frequently creep in when several words come between the subject and verb—or when the subject comes at the end of the sentence rather than at the beginning (the typical place).

Incorrect: *The group of financial planners, brokers, investors, and other dignitaries always hesitate to make a solid commitment on new policies while the meeting is in session.*

Correct: *The group of financial planners, brokers, investors, and other dignitaries always hesitates to make a solid commitment on new policies while the meeting is in session.*

Incorrect: *There at the tradeshow last week in Chicago was exhibit booths perfect for our products next year.*

Correct: *There at the tradeshow last week in Chicago were exhibit booths perfect for our products next year.*

Pick the Right Pronoun

An example of the most egregious pronoun error appeared in my inbox a couple of weeks ago from an email marketer. The first line began, "During the hot summer months, *me and my team* would like to encourage you to . . ." How embarrassing for this writer!

I Versus Me

Me and my team? Two problems here. First, *me* can never ever, never ever, never ever be the subject of a sentence. No, not ever! When choosing between *me* or *I* as the subject in *any* sentence, *I* is the correct choice.

Second, don't be boorish by putting yourself before others. Correct constructions are *my team and I, Mindy and I,* or *the client and I.* If you invited these people as your guests for dinner, you wouldn't rush through the buffet line ahead of them, would you? I didn't think so. So don't push yourself to the front of the phrase. You'll always be correct naming the other people first.

Now about the proper use of *me*: Because this is a pronoun in the objective case, it serves as the "object" of something in the sentence: a direct object, an indirect object, or the object of a preposition.

Give me your thoughts about this contract.

The client sent the guidelines for developing their system to Bryan and me.

My boss is waiting for Tami and me to interview the top three candidates.

Here's a little trick to help you always remember to choose *me* in these slots: Leave out the other people and say the sentence to yourself. Your ear will help you choose correctly. For example, with the sentences above, you would never say:

The client sent the guidelines for developing their system to I.

My boss is waiting for I to interview the top three candidates.

Myself/Me

The "self" pronouns are called reflexive or intensifying pronouns. That term is descriptive, meaning these pronouns reflect back on someone already mentioned in the sentence and emphasize that person.

He himself, not a staff member, signed the contract.

We ourselves like the investment, but our silent partner is still undecided about moving forward.

I myself trust Matt to handle the project, but my boss does not.

The most frequent error with a reflexive pronoun is using *myself* when you need the simple *me*.

Incorrect: *The dietary supplements prescribed for Amy and myself have been helpful.*
Correct: *The dietary supplements prescribed for Amy and me have been helpful.*

Incorrect: *The manager has suggested additional training for the leadership team and myself.*
Correct: *The manager has suggested additional training for the leadership team and me.*

He/Him, She/Her, We/Us, They/Them

He, she, we, and *they* are subjective pronouns. They serve as subjects in a sentence. *Him, her, us,* and *them* are objective pronouns. They serve as objects in a sentence (direct object, indirect object, or object of a preposition).

If you don't remember the parts of speech and how they function in a sentence, here's an easy trick: Again, just leave the other people out of the sentence and choose the pronoun that sounds right. You'll be correct 99 percent of the time.

Incorrect: *Jeff told Marisa and I that the mutual fund might suspend or postpone the repurchase order.*

Correct: *Jeff told Marisa and me that the mutual fund might suspend or postpone the repurchase order.*

> [Leave out the other people: You would never say "Jeff told I that the . . ."]

Incorrect: *Headquarters staff recommends that Bev, Andres, and us review the tax return before filing.*
Correct: *Headquarters staff recommends that Bev, Andres, and we review the tax return before filing.*

> [Leave out the other people: You would never say "Headquarters staff recommends that us review the tax return . . ."]

Incorrect: *The supervisor has suggested that we keep this just between Terry, you, and I.*
Correct: *The supervisor has suggested that we keep this just between Terry, you, and me.*

> [Leave out the other people: "The supervisor has suggested that we keep this just between I . . ." In this example, "I" is a subjective pronoun. When two or more people are meant, the equivalent subjective pronoun is "we." Your ear would never let you say "between we." You'd say "between us." So use the equivalent objective pronoun, "me."]

Punctuate Properly

How passionate are you about punctuation? The following note in this exact form is from the office of a financial advisor:

> *Hi Harmeet Can you let me know your availability for a meeting with Ed before he leaves for New Orleans he'll be gone all of next week for a conference and would like to get this arranged before he leaves please let me know and I'll confirm with him and get back to you in the meantime I'd like to discuss the immediate changes you wanted me to make in your accounts.*

Four complete sentences punctuated as one! The reasons people make such egregious punctuation errors vary.

- **Unknowledgeable:** They don't know what they don't know. (But just because *they* don't know better doesn't mean others don't know, don't notice, and don't care!)

- **Apathetic:** These writers consider punctuation a "minor" matter. Likewise, some would consider salt on food a minor issue. But leave it out altogether, and notice the taste—or should I say, the blandness.

- **Careless:** They're working too fast.

- **Smartphone lazy:** Having the punctuation keys on a second screen does make adding punctuation time-consuming. But then so is brushing your teeth.

Having the punctuation keys on a second screen
does make adding punctuation time-consuming.
But then so is brushing your teeth.

So why pay attention when punctuating your prose? Three reasons: clarity, image, and speed.

Punctuation Affects Clarity

Let's say your boss emails you: *"How's it going with the Gleason account? Do you think you can close the deal with your next meeting?"*

You respond: *"For whatever reason they're silent."*

Your boss is going to think she got an incomplete response. She'll be left wondering, "So what did you start to say about their silence?" Because of the missing comma, this response sounds like a spurt of words—an incomplete thought. But punctuated correctly, it would be clear: *"For whatever reason, they're silent."*

Now let's get to the most problematic punctuation error of all—the misuse of commas. To be dramatic about it, cut a

Bad grammar affects clarity, image, and speed.

comma and you may destroy someone's career or cost your organization millions of dollars. Court cases have turned on comma confusion.

The comma challenge basically comes down to this: What people do intuitively when speaking often bewilders them when writing. Punctuation helps you translate voice inflection to the page.

Let me be more specific: A comma tells a reader to pause. The absence of a comma means that a reader should keep going full speed ahead. If you set off the middle or final part of a sentence with a comma, you're telling a reader that part of the statement is nonessential—that it *adds* information but is not essential to the meaning of what preceded it.

If you can't remove that part of the sentence without changing the meaning of what's left of the statement, then don't set that part off with commas.

Let's try that principle: *"Silvia submitted our proposal, which has a strong chance of winning, to the Bahrain client last week."*

Question: Do you need a comma to set off the *which* clause?

Apply the rule: Omit the *which* clause to determine if the meaning of the rest of the sentence changes without it: *"Silvia submitted our proposal to the Bahrain client last week."* The meaning of what remains doesn't change. Result: The enclosing commas to set off that clause *"which has a strong chance of winning"* are used correctly. That *which* clause provides only additional information about the *proposal*, but doesn't change the meaning.

Consider how you would inflect your voice and where you would pause in the following sentences. (Although I'm certainly not suggesting that you learn to punctuate by voice inflection, that system *will* help you determine the meaning in your own sentences and understand the use of commas to set off nonessential clauses.)

Correct Comma Choices—
But Different Meanings

We knew the couple who bought my dad's home.
> [Essential information: The "who" clause indicates which couple. No comma.]

That operation is located in the North, where we have very few labor shortages.
> [The comma setting the "where" clause off from the rest of the sentence tells you this is nonessential information: The "where" clause just adds information about their locations in the North, but doesn't distinguish one part of the North from another.]

That operation is located in the North where we have very few labor shortages.
> [The absence of a comma restricts the meaning of the North. It distinguishes one specific location in the North from other northern locations. Since that clause is essential to the meaning of the North, do not use a comma to set off this essential information.]

According to this contract, which Joe had not seen until this morning, we have 30 days to pay the invoice.

[Nonessential information: The "which" clause just adds extra information about the contract but does not distinguish it from other contracts. Use commas to set it off.]

The host explained the format that the panel would follow during the second debate.

[Essential information: The "that" clause tells which format. Because this information is essential to the meaning of "format," do not use commas to set it off.]

Here's a rule of thumb for essential and nonessential clauses that involve *that* and *which*:

- *Which* clauses add nonessential information. Use commas to set that information off from the rest of the sentence.

- *That* clauses provide essential information. Don't use commas to cut that information off from the rest of the sentence.

Court cases have turned on comma confusion.

Improper Punctuation Tarnishes Your Image

"Carelessness with punctuation is symptomatic of inattention to detail in general," according to the CEO of one of our Fortune 100 clients in the financial services industry. "To our customers, such errors mean that we don't amortize their loans correctly." Comments like that from C-suite executives should make professionals take more care in the emails they zap off to coworkers every day—emails that have a long life.

Common errors like the following cause readers to do a double-take:

I agree Michelle that it's a good idea.
>[Use a comma to set off a name when you address someone. "I agree, Michelle, that it's a good idea."]

You'll love the tips in this article; by Jake.
>[A semicolon separates two complete thoughts. "By Jake" is not a complete thought. Here, it sounds like a byline or a swear phrase.]

We have 3 employee's going!
>[An apostrophe shows possession— not the case here. "Employees" is the proper plural form.]

I'm pulling no punches here: Just as with traffic signs, punctuation marks give specific directions to the reader. Using them incorrectly looks as goofy as someone who honks a horn every time they turn left, uses their left turn signal to turn right, and drives with their headlights on high beam at noon. Drivers who use the wrong signals pose a safety hazard. Emails with the wrong punctuation pose a clarity problem.

If you want to be a clear communicator, get passionate about punctuation.

Drivers who use the wrong signals pose a safety hazard. Emails with the wrong punctuation pose a clarity problem.

The Runaway Exclamation Point. One more caution about punctuation: Rein in the runaway exclamation point. A sentence should end with ONE punctuation mark: a period, a question mark, or an exclamation point. But again, social media and texting habits have overflowed into casual emails. To mimic the emotion, casual emailers have grown exuberant, tossing exclamation points like confetti at the ends of sentences: *I hope the convention lives up to all your expectations!!!*

When expressing a negative emotion, runaway exclamation points make you sound as though you're having a meltdown: *I think putting "Compliance" issues on the agenda for Tuesday's meeting with the client is totally inappropriate at this early stage!!!!*

For serious emails, one exclamation point will do the job.

Casual emailers have grown exuberant,
tossing exclamation points like confetti
at the ends of sentences.

For the email writer, grammar presents a broad enough minefield for an entire book. In fact, I've written two on that topic alone. If you think grammar in general and punctuation in particular might be tarnishing your personal brand every time you hit SEND, grab a copy of *Booher's Rules of Business Grammar: 101 Fast and Easy Ways to Correct the Most Common Errors* (McGraw-Hill).

Bad grammar is like bad breath—even your best friends won't tell you.

EDIT FOR STYLE

From the earlier discussion of the MADE Format™, you might have inferred that email is no place for friendly chit-chat. Not so. Just like face-to-face communication, email can serve to build rapport and relationships. In those cases, you'll use an informal style. But even coworkers you know well have the task of tackling their inbox. Reading lengthy rambles takes time away from other projects that must get done before your reader can get back to family, hobbies, vacation, sleep, or whatever.

So as you edit for style, consider not only your relationship, but also your topic, tone, and purpose.

Your tone: You don't want to sound gruff when sending a client an invitation to your tradeshow booth. But you don't necessarily want to sound chatty when emailing a vendor for the third time to complain about being overcharged.

Greetings and closings contribute most strongly to the tone. Addressing someone by their first name sets up an informal, friendly tone, whereas using the last name suggests a formal tone. Omitting the name altogether conveys impersonality.

Also consider how the closing contributes to the tone.

Informal Closings	More Formal Closings
All the best	*Best wishes*
Best	*With gratitude*
Cordially	*Thank you*
Cheers	*Thank you very much*
Warm regards	*Thank you for your help*
Good luck	*Regards*
Talk soon	*Sincerely*
Thanks	*Yours truly*
Hugs	

If your closing line almost types itself,
delete the cliché to ensure a fresh, personal style.

Your topic. If you have a simple topic, your word choices and sentence patterns will likely be informal. If your topic is complex, your word choice may be technical and your sentence patterns may be more formal.

Your relationship to the reader. If you know your reader well, you'll likely be less formal and make some assumptions about their understanding of a situation. When writing to a wide audience, however, take a more formal approach and provide adequate detail so your message doesn't generate more questions than answers.

Your purpose. Consider how your email might be used long-term. Will it be forwarded to an outside expert—an attorney, an accountant, a government official—for review, input, protest, filing, or response? Will it be used as an ongoing reference? Even if you know the recipient well, its purpose might be significant and suggest a more formal approach.

With all the above in mind, be intentional. Edit your email until you have the appropriate style for the situation. For example, compare the emails in examples 15–17.

Friendly/Informal

Trainees,

Congratulations on completing the 2-day "Leadership for Non-Supervisors."

As a follow-up to the training, let your boss know you're interested in taking on more responsibility. Volunteer for special projects whenever you have the time. Never turn down the chance to work with other people you don't know well and typically don't interact with. Every experience like this gives you a chance to toot your own horn and add to your tool kit. You never know when one of these new

(continued on next page)

Friendly/Informal *(continued)*

contacts can put you onto a totally new career path you've never considered.

Again, congrats on completing the course!

Best,
Deepak

EXAMPLE 15. A friendly style works for most situations within your organization.

Formal

Trainees,

Congratulations on completing the 2-day course "Leadership for Non-Supervisors."

As a follow-up to the program, we suggest that you look for opportunities to let your supervisor know of your interest in taking on more responsibility. Volunteer for special projects. Never turn down the opportunity to work with others outside your department whom you do not interact with routinely. Every experience like this gives you a chance to show your talents and add to your skill set. You never know when one of these colleagues can introduce you to a new career path inside the organization.

Once again, congratulations on your achievement.

Yours in service,
Your Training Team

EXAMPLE 16. Use a formal style for a wide audience, for those outside your organization, and particularly for sensitive topics and serious situations.

Frivolous

Hey!

Congrats on completing the 2-day course "Leadership for Non-Supervisors."

So what now that you're back on the job? Bored? Tired of cranking it out every day in a job you hate? Tell your boss you've got the itch to move on. Raise your hand for some special project if you can find time. You never know— you may find some kindred souls in other departments, people you don't usually run into. So toot your own horn. Whatever it takes to get noticed. You never know when one of these dudes can put you onto a totally new lead— one that can eventually move you to the 65th floor!

We've got your back!

Andy

EXAMPLE 17. This frivolous style is not appropriate for a business email going to a wide, diverse audience.

Both the informal and the formal versions are appropriate for email. But unless you're writing to a coworker you know very well, forget the frivolous version altogether for your work email.

■ ■ ■

After you've edited for clarity, conciseness, grammar, and style, you can hit SEND with confidence.

CHAPTER 5

Organize Folders and Files to Save and Send Information

> One of the advantages of being disorganized is
> that one is always having surprising discoveries.
>
> —**A. A. MILNE,** English author and creator
>   of the popular Winnie-the-Pooh series

> I have files, I have computer files, and, you know,
> files on paper. But most of it is really in my head.
> So God help me if anything ever happens to my head!
>
> —**GEORGE R. R. MARTIN,** American novelist
>   and TV producer

Consider how much time you waste because you need to attach a file or find other information to respond to email requests—information or files stored "somewhere." According to the UNC survey, 40 percent of knowledge workers say they spend more than fifteen minutes a day searching for files or information either to include or attach as they reply to email. Seven percent spend more than an hour a day searching for information or files.

A colleague of mine recently posted in a closed Facebook group of more than 900 members a comment something like this: "Can someone tell me a keyword to search on my PC to find a file about the IRS guidelines on how to classify contractors and full-time employees? I've just spent more than an hour looking for that file! I can't remember the title or where

I could have filed it, but I know I have it somewhere. I've searched under XXXXXX and YYYYY and that didn't bring anything up. What else could I have called it? Can somebody suggest other keywords to search?"

At some time or other, most of us have been that searcher seeking a lost file or folder. Some have then improved their organizing system for the better.

Tackle this organizing challenge and you'll solve a big part of your email problem.

If your files are set up in a totally different way from what I'm about to suggest, you may need to devote a half-day to reorganize them. But I guarantee that you'll recoup that time in a matter of a few weeks from your increased speed in relocating information.

Restructuring and company buy-outs have necessitated this major file organization four times during my career. Three of the four times, I took a time-out and set up the framework. Each time-out took approximately three to four hours. Within days, my time-saving paid huge dividends for me and for others on the team.

Another option: If you decide not to devote three to four hours now to reorganizing, at least set up the new folder and subfolder framework for your documents going forward. Then, as you use files one by one, move them to the new, correct location. (This second option can be slightly more confusing during the transition but it does work.)

STREAMLINE FOLDERS AND FILES AND NAME THEM FUNCTIONALLY

No matter your company size or industry, you need just four primary folders (or, if you're a large enterprise, you may make these different directories):

Teams/Users (*Subfolders are team members/users.*)

Offerings: Projects, Services, or Products
(*Subfolders are your team's output.*)

Clients *(Subfolders here are internal or external clients.)*

Administration *(Subfolders here are company or department operational files.)*

If you need an acronym or "saying" to remember this structure, here it is: "The **team** offers **products and services** to **clients** and then **administers** them."

That saying works similarly to the mnemonic **E**very **G**ood **B**oy **D**oes **F**ine, which helps piano players recall the notes on a musical staff, or like **METT** (**M**ission, **E**nemy, **T**errain/weather, **T**roops/equipment), which soldiers use to determine their course of action in a combat situation.

For example, with the above four primary folders, your files might look like the following if your output primarily goes *outside* your organization:

Teams/Users
  Jordan
  Kimberly
  Minjoo
Offerings: Projects, Services, or Products
  Alzheimer's or Other Dementia Care
  Hospice Support
  Personal Care Services: Transportation, Errands, Mobility
Clients
  Doctors' Offices
  Emergency Care Clinics
  Hospital Systems
  Individuals
Administration
  Benefits
  Conferences, Webinars (Notes)
  Financials
  Forms
  IT
  Meeting Agendas (Monthly, Staff)

Policies and Procedures
Status Reports
Suppliers
Training
Webcasts (by CEO)

If Michael works as a researcher and grant writer for his organization with his output going primarily to internal clients, then his folders and files might differ significantly:

Teams/Users
Bedford Test Team
Rockwall Bohart Redesign Team
Springfield Research Review Team
Offerings: Projects, Services, or Products
Articles—For Conferences
Articles—For Publication
Grants Approved
Grants Requested
Surveys—Completed
Surveys—Pending
Clients
Clinical Staff
Marketing Team
Pharmaceutical Staff
Administration
Benefits
Forms
Meeting Agendas (Monthly, Staff)
Policies and Procedures
Status Reports
Training

Notice that the subfolders under the "Administration" folder are similar—whether your output goes inside or outside your organization.

On occasion you may run into a situation where a file

could reasonably belong in more than one category. When such overlapping is the situation with any particular file, place the file in the *first* applicable folder. Then all you have to remember is the order of the four categories: "The **team** offers **projects, services, and products** to **clients** and then **administers** them."

BEAT THE ALPHABET FOR CONVENIENCE'S SAKE

Because email systems automatically alphabetize folders, the ones you want may be located in the middle of the list and may not be easy to locate quickly. To override that forced alphabetizing, you can opt to pull your most frequently used folders to the top of the list for quick access. Here's how.

Use Punctuation or Numerals to Move Folders to the Front

Use exclamation marks—either one, two, or three—to force a folder to move to the front of the A titles, like this:

> **Administration**
> !Forms
> Applications
> Benefits
> Bios
> Conferences, Webinars (Notes)
> Financials
> IT
> Meeting Agendas (Monthly, Staff)

If you want a second group of files or folders to move up to follow the "Forms" folder, use two exclamation points:

> **Administration**
> !Forms
> !!Suppliers (Current)
> 1—Training
> 2—Status Reports
> Applications

Benefits
Conferences, Webinars (Notes)
Financials
IT
Meeting Agendas (Monthly, Staff)
Policies and Procedures

Catch Some ZZZ's to Kick Items to the End of the Line

To override the automatic alphabetizing, group several folders together, and move them to the end of a long list, start the titles with one, two, or three Z's. Like this:

Status Reports
Suppliers
Training & Webcasts
Z—Forms
ZZ—Applications
ZZZ—Guidelines

ARCHIVE FOLDERS TO MOVE FILES OUT OF THE WAY

If you've decided to set up new folders going forward (but want to keep your old folders as they are currently arranged until you have time to sort through them and delete or move them to the new place), you can use the following workaround for the transition period.

Create a folder called "Z—Archived as of [Date]." Then move all your current folders under this folder. As you need a file, find it in the "Archived as of [Date]" section and then move it to the correct new place.

Keep in mind that this is *not* the most efficient way to reorganize your folders. At first you'll find yourself having to check two places for a file: in the Archived section and in the new section. But eventually, all the folders you frequently use will get moved over to what is now the current section. Then only those you rarely use will be left in the Archived section.

At some point, you can take half an hour and either move all those remaining in the Archived section into the correct place or delete them if they're no longer useful.

CREATE FOLDER TEMPLATES AS A SHORT-CUT

To save even more time, you can systematize subfolders once and for all by creating a folder template, with the subfolders inside. As an example, here's a folder template for training courses. You could simply copy this primary folder (with the subfolders inside) and then change the title for each training program. Presto, you're good to go for organizing all new course files.

Oil Rig Safety Course
    Administration
    Job Aids
    Leader Guide
    Participant Materials
    Slideshows

USE THE "GENRE" CONCEPT FOR CONSISTENCY

Trying to locate inconsistently titled files represents another huge time-waster.

An account executive in my financial advisor's office used to send me three routine monthly reports titled differently each time they arrived. For the first few months, I saved these reports with his random titles, thinking they were something different each month—only to discover they were the same periodic reports with the "title du jour":

BooherTramcoDate
TramcoBooherDate
Date—Tramco—PortfolioPerformance—Booher
Booher—PortfolioPerformance—Tramco—Date
MonthlyPerformance_Booher_Date_Tramco

Title folders and files consistently.

To prevent this time-waster, when titling folders and files, use the "Genre" concept. To illustrate: If you're buying books at an online store, you move through the directory like this: Books > Nonfiction > Business > Communication > Writing > [Specific Book Title].

When selecting a movie, you move through the directory like this:

Classics > Romance > Comedy > [Specific Movie Title]
Drama > Action/Thriller > [Specific Movie Title]

Likewise, when titling your folders or files, think in this same "genre" format: Solar System > Earth > Country > State > City. This "genre" titling concept will help you align your documents for quickly scanning and grabbing the file you need to attach to your emails. Examples:

Audit—Bellview—Assignments
Audit—Bellview—Results
Audit—Redrock—Assignments
Audit—Redrock—Results
Forms—Expense Reports
Forms—W9s

Forms—579 Authorization—Requesting
Forms—579 Authorization—Granting
Forms—579 Authorization—Declining

Dates and linking between words can be troublesome with this otherwise smooth genre concept for titling folders and files. Here are all the variations that create kinks in an otherwise straightforward organizational plan:

- Dates written *randomly* as day-month-year, month-day-year, or year-month-day, plus dates in the 6-digit format versus the 4-digit format
- Dates *before* document titles
- Dates *after* document titles
- Words linked by *underscore* symbol
- Words separated by a *period*
- Words separated by a *hyphen*
- Words separated by a *space hyphen space*
- Words written together, each word having an initial cap

Take your choice with the above patterns, but be consistent. Consistency allows similar documents to align and alphabetize properly for quick scanning so you can grab what you need easily—or see what's missing. The preference on dates is to start with the four-digit year so the months fall into place sequentially:

Capital Expenditures Planned—2020-06-30
Capital Expenditures Planned—2022-03-31
Capital Expenditures Planned—2024-09-30
Capital Expenditures Planned—2026-03-30
Capital Expenditures Planned—2028-06-30

■ ■ ■

Setting up your folders (and titling files consistently) may take you a few hours. But when you're finished, you'll recoup your investment many times over as you handle email going forward.

CHAPTER 6

Protect Yourself and Your Organization

> Every time you write an email, it is in the
> public domain. There are all these ways where
> security is not as good as people believe.
>
> —**PETER THIEL**, cofounder of PayPal,
>   venture capitalist, philanthropist, and author

Y ou don't want this to happen to you: Lynn (not her real
name) lost $8,000 from her checking account through
a rather unique scam pulled off by a clever identity theft
ring. Here's how it happened.

Lynn gets a call from the toll-free number of her financial
services firm (let's call them RWA), through which she has a
mortgage, savings and checking accounts, and a debit card.
The very professional, articulate woman on the phone follows
RWA's customary protocol regarding outreach and member
verification. She identifies herself as an agent of the Fraud Department, calling due to a fraud alert on Lynn's account regarding charges that seem to be outside her normal spending
patterns. The RWA agent asks Lynn if she has charged $142 at
Walmart in LA or has purchased a $628 one-way ticket from
LAX.

Alarmed, Lynn tells the RWA agent that these are defi-
nitely unauthorized charges. So the agent proceeds with the
process to cancel Lynn's credit card and issue a replacement
card.

As part of the process, the agent confirms Lynn's address and asks her to verify the 3-digit code on her debit card.

At that request, Lynn feels uncomfortable giving that information without more verification from the agent that she is indeed an authorized RWA agent. So the agent confirms more information about Lynn, specifically her date of birth and her social security number.

After the RWA agent reassures her with that further personal information, Lynn gives the agent the 3-digit code on her debit card. The agent then instructs Lynn to discard her current debit card and to expect a new one via Federal Express the next day.

Five minutes later, Lynn receives another call from the same RWA toll-free number from the same agent. She advises Lynn that there is one more step before she can overnight the new debit card: She needs to send Lynn a text message with a security code, and Lynn is to read it back to her.

Lynn does as she is told to complete the verification process and get her replacement credit and debit card. They end the call.

Within minutes, Lynn starts getting text alerts from the *real* RWA about withdrawals from her account: 10 ATM transactions of $800 each. Initially, Lynn thinks these alerts involve the same "unauthorized charges" the "fraud agent" called her about just a few minutes earlier.

But growing more uneasy, Lynn calls RWA's Fraud Department directly. The real RWA fraud representative confirms her fears: RWA did not call her to report suspicious activity. There are no fraudulent Walmart or LAX charges on her account.

At that point, Lynn learns the unfortunate truth: She has been scammed.

Since the scamming incident, with the help of RWA's investigative team, Lynn has discovered how the thief managed to pull off this scam. Someone had been calling RWA by spoofing Lynn's mobile number for weeks leading up to this event. Each time the person called RWA, they attempted to get past certain security barriers. Eventually, over time and with several calls, the identity thief found someone at RWA willing to give out tidbits of Lynn's personal information and allow her to increase the ATM withdrawal limit without RWA's 2-step authentication process.

Lynn also learned that her debit card had been swiped by a third party (indicating an identity theft ring). A duplicate "scan card" was manufactured so that it could be used at an ATM.

While much of the scam happened by phone, some of the interaction happened by email and text—particularly within RWA. And even the phone interactions with the thief *could* conceivably have been pulled off by text and email had that been the thief's channel of choice (more about that later).

For now, the point needs no repetition: Cyberspace is shark-infested, and email accounts provide chum. As a user, your chances of becoming a victim are high. According to the UNC survey, 28 percent of respondents reported being a victim of an email scam. Here are the various ways they were scammed (the numbers total more than 100 percent because some victims were scammed more than once).

33% Clicking on a link in an email

28% Opening an attachment

27% Opening an email from a sender they
thought they recognized

10% Through a combination of email, text,
and phone

27% Having an email account hacked

Cyberspace is shark-infested,
and email accounts provide chum.

DOUBLE-CHECK THE SENDER'S EMAIL ADDRESS

You are your best defense in protecting your own email. You've heard the caution, "Don't open emails or click on links from people you don't know." That warning doesn't get specific enough.

Hackers and thieves have become snoopers, using social media to pilfer and "borrow" your friends' names. So even when you recognize the email sender's name, check out the domain name in the email address. Verify that there's not a period, apostrophe, comma, double letter, or some other strange symbol at the beginning or end of their name or domain name in the email address.

Unfortunately, I have my own email scam story to add to the annals of email scams and Internet thievery. Here's how the thief grabbed my credit card by email—during the writing of this book, no less! (Believe me when I say I'm a skeptical soul—but one who was in a big hurry that day.)

A month before the incident, a friend of mine (I'll call her Jena Storm) had her email address spoofed. Someone emailed me as "Jena Storm," sending me a link to a party invitation that week. I knew it wasn't on the up and up because the real Jena was out of the country. So I let my friend Jena know about the incident, assuming she would investigate and then change her address and/or password immediately.

A month later (the morning of the scam), Jena and I are commenting back and forth on Facebook about food and diets—a typical topic for us. I mention that I want to lose seven pounds before a big conference—but that I've had houseguests over the weekend and have been cooking and eating far too much!

A few minutes later an email from "Jena Storm" pops into my inbox with this cryptic message: "Interested in this?" (followed by a link).

I glance at the three-word message, remembering our earlier Facebook "conversation," and click. It's an ad for a supplement. Although I've never in my life bought such a product,

Check incoming email for smudged images, odd lettering, unfamiliar domains, and poor grammar.

I thought, "Why not?" Jena buys supplements all the time. After all, the site looks professional and is loaded with testimonials from well-known people. Within two minutes of inputting my card number, I do a double-take of Jena's email address. It's her name all right, but a different domain. I text my friend: "What's your new email address after you got spoofed or hacked or whatever on vacation?"

"I haven't changed it yet. No one else mentioned that they got a bad email from me. . . . Sorry."

The sinking feeling hit in the pit of my stomach. I immediately called my credit card company to cancel the card. Scammed and cancelled all within about four minutes. Next time I may not be so fortunate.

So to repeat the warning: Stay alert! Call an organization or a friend directly if the email name or domain name in the address looks odd for any reason.

A hacker's email may look strange for any number of reasons. A dead giveaway is the grammar: Typically, articles (*the, a, an*) are missing, and verb tenses are incorrect. Logos and other images may look a little "off." The email address may look exact—except for an apostrophe or comma at the beginning or a double letter in the center that's almost unnoticeable at a glance.

Instead of clicking the link or calling the number in the email, look up the actual number from your own directory to see if the company has actually sent such a document. Typically, they'll have a special mailbox where you can forward the questionable email so they can investigate.

Last, keep in mind that just because an organization or individual has a profile on LinkedIn or Twitter with a few thousand followers doesn't guarantee that he or she won't email you a link taking you to dangerous places. Your sender may not even be aware that the link included in his or her marketing email leads to a site that has been recently infected. Landing on one of these sites can lead to a very bad day.

One other scary—and embarrassing—thought before we leave this topic: Having your email account hacked and not knowing it! On several occasions, I've received an email from a hacked friend's account that read something like this: *"Dianna, As you may have heard, I've been on a speaking tour in East Africa for the past 3 months. I got sick while there and was hospitalized. (Long story) But just as I was being released, I discovered that my passport and all my belongings had been stolen. Unable to connect with anyone on the outside at the moment. Could you wire $200 to XXXXXX so that I can get transportation to the nearest embassy. Will call as soon as I'm back in the States."* (Only the details vary in these emails.)

Within hours—but sometimes days—the real owner of the email account sends the follow-up message: *"Sorry about the earlier email. I've been hacked. I'm quite healthy, have my passport in my pocket, and am safe and sound in Des Moines."*

If you're in doubt about whether your email account has been hacked, check your SENT folder for any nefarious emails. You may have to check that folder on your local machine and at the server level. That doesn't mean, of course, that the hacker has sent out emails under your address. The hacker may simply be snooping around in your email for other information, such as credit card numbers or bank account information. (Doesn't that make you feel better?)

BEWARE ATTACHMENTS—YOURS AND THEIRS

For years, reporters have not accepted pitches, articles, or press releases (even hot news stories) as attachments. Their routine email auto-response: "Please copy any attachments you're sending into the body of your email and resend."

Shocked because they intend to send along a long press release or story, the emailer responds to that notice: "But this release is 800 words, two full, single-spaced pages."

The reporter replies again: "That's fine. Please copy and paste it into the body of your email."

Point made. Attachments deliver viruses of the very worst kind.

INSTALL ANTIVIRUS AND ANTI-MALWARE PROGRAMS

According to the UNC survey, roughly three-fourths (73 percent) of email users are *unprotected!* Although 41 percent of the respondents report that they do have an antivirus software program installed, that's not enough in today's environment. While antivirus programs serve as a first line of defense against common viruses, anti-malware protects against much more: viruses, malicious software, spyware, adware, ransomware, trojans, worms, and the like.

You need both antivirus and anti-malware programs installed on any computer where you access email (popular programs include Bitdefender, Norton, Trend Micro, McAfee, Webroot, and Kaspersky). And after you've paused the software for some reason, such as investigating a compatibility issue, click the "Auto-restart after X minutes" button. Never trust your own memory to restart the protection program.

CREATE UNIQUE PASSWORDS

Each year, various security experts publish lists of the most frequently used passwords. Here's SplashData's *Top 25 Passwords* on the last available list:

1.	123456 (unchanged)	14.	login (down 3)
2.	Password (unchanged)	15.	abc123 (down 1)
3.	12345678 (up 1)	16.	starwars (new)
4.	qwerty (up 2)	17.	123123 (new)
5.	12345 (down 2)	18.	dragon (up 1)
6.	123456789 (new)	19.	passw0rd (down 1)
7.	letmein (new)	20.	master (up 1)
8.	1234567 (unchanged)	21.	hello (new)
9.	football (down 4)	22.	freedom (new)
10.	iloveyou (new)	23.	whatever (new)
11.	admin (up 4)	24.	qazwsx (new)
12.	welcome (unchanged)	25.	trustno1 (new)
13.	monkey (new)		

Add to this Top 25 list other common words from pop culture or the hit movies of the year or decade and you've just about maxed out your colleagues' creativity. It will take hackers only seconds to hack these passwords. If you're serious about security, you have to do better than your uncreative colleagues.

While 45 percent of the UNC respondents say they do use unique passwords for each email account, that leaves 55 percent who do not. If you fall into this less creative or less-motivated group, here's help. Consider the characteristics of strong passwords:

- Long (up to the maximum your system will allow)
- A combination of upper- and lowercase letters, numerals, and special characters
- Unique to each email account, site, or server where you log in
- Unique to you

Given these specs, how do you create—and remember—unique email log-ons if you have multiple email accounts and change passwords frequently? Or dozens or even hundreds of passwords for other accounts? Develop a scheme for creating new passwords. For example:

- The first letters of the first five words of a song, nursery rhyme, movie title, or poem (*I Will Always Love You* by Whitney Houston, the top movie song of all time = IWALY)
- Your brother's initials in caps (THJ)
- Your best friend's birth year
- Two symbols (##)

Or whatever. Create your own password scheme. Then when you change your log-on password from time to time, change the "song" component or the symbols. You get the idea.

Then, after going to the trouble to be creative, don't be careless. Keep your passwords safe. Log off when you leave your computer unattended. Set a password on your screensaver and activate it.

CHANGE PASSWORDS FREQUENTLY

With a system similar to what's detailed above, remembering your log-ons proves easier. But if you're logging into multiple email accounts (the average user has more than 3.7 email accounts, according to the UNC survey) plus all other accounts, you'll need something beyond your memory to enable you to change passwords frequently. Once again, survey responses suggest a lax attitude about security: The largest group (38 percent) change passwords only when prompted or forced to do so.

Use a password manager (like LastPass, Dashlane, Log-MeIn, or 1Password) to keep all your passwords safe and manage them easily. You'll have only *one* password to remember.

These programs will generate a unique password for you for each account if you prefer to use their computer-generated passwords. However, security experts report that hackers get past those system-generated passwords faster than your own unique ones. So here's the best idea: Create unique passwords for your accounts based on your own devised scheme. Then use a password manager to store and remember the unique passwords for you.

USE TWO-STEP AUTHENTICATION WHERE POSSIBLE

Some users complain about the added time required to gain access with a two-step authentication process. But when compared to the time needed to deal with a stolen ID, the extra time for prevention is minuscule.

USE MULTIPLE EMAIL ACCOUNTS

Set up different email accounts for different purposes. Handle your banking and investments from one account. Do online shopping and credit-card purchases with a separate account. Use disposable addresses for other purposes such as downloading freebies. Keep a general email account for your personal or family correspondence. If one account gets hacked, that limits the damage of what a hacker can learn to that single account.

SEGMENT YOUR NETWORK

At home, segment your Wi-Fi network into three areas: one for guests, one for kids, and another for adults. Otherwise, any guest in your home can pick up your Internet traffic and potentially see your passwords as you log on. If you are not technically proficient enough to do that, follow the steps the service provider typically shows on its website. Another option: Watch a YouTube video to learn how.

REMEMBER THAT EMAIL "LIVES" FOREVER

If we have learned one thing from political and corporate scandals, it's this: Emails don't go away when deleted. They live forever either on a hard drive (until it's wiped clean), on an organization's server, or in cloud storage. And if that's not enough places to worry about, some colleague probably got copied along the way and has a backup stored.

So assume that whatever you write in an email may eventually be read by others who may not be pleased. If it's derogatory, your words could jeopardize your job or ruin you financially. Examples fill the news almost daily of corporate and nonprofit executives who've been dismissed when their emails containing sexual innuendoes, racial slurs, or unpopular political views surfaced.

Think twice—or five times—about emails you write or documents you forward on company systems. In particular, concern yourself with comments about suppliers, potential suppliers, or clients. They owe you no loyalty.

Should an ugly situation arise at work about which you've offered comments in an email, you could be in for some sleepless nights and grueling days.

CHAPTER 7

Maintain Your Professional Reputation

> For email, the old postcard rule applies. Nobody else is supposed to read your postcards, but you'd be a fool if you write anything private on one.
>
> —**JUDITH MARTIN,** American journalist and etiquette expert, better known by her pen name, Miss Manners

> Emails get reactions. Phone calls start conversations.
>
> —**SIMON SINEK,** British-American author, speaker, and consultant

Your personal brand is reflected primarily in how you express yourself in conversation, in meetings, and in writing. Consider how much of your "conversation" happens through email. For many professionals, your communication is how you "show up" in today's marketplace; it's how you "do" your work.

In addition to your tone, topics, and word choices, consider these further guidelines to protect your personal image.

BEWARE OF LIABILITY FOR LEGITIMATE QUESTIONS AND STATEMENTS

Emails containing offensive remarks that appear on company equipment or servers make both the organization and you personally liable. Copyright violations aside, personal liability for email misuse involves misstatements, slander, defamation, harassment, and the like.

But your legal awareness has to go beyond those obvious disasters. Other potential liabilities might involve:

- Straightforward questions
- Inconsistent meeting dates
- Inconsistent distribution lists
- Inaction or nonresponses to email warnings

Let me get more specific on these email potholes.

Big lawsuits (think pharmaceutical companies, auto manufacturers, medical device manufacturers, healthcare facilities, construction companies) involving personal injury often center on an email where someone has raised a simple question.

Imagine a scenario where someone dies in an auto accident. The victim's family sues the auto manufacturer, saying the brakes on the new model were faulty. Your email simply raised this question very early in the manufacturing process: *"Should we do more testing on the XYZ system before moving on to the next stage?"* That email may be used as court evidence for a charge of neglect or cost-cutting on the part of the manufacturer. Yet your original question might not have been intended as a warning at all. Perhaps you had no concern that there might be a safety issue, but instead were simply asking about when to schedule the next phase.

Of course, you need to ask straightforward questions in emails. But never couch cautions and recommendations in timid questions. If you have concerns, state them directly and persuasively. The point is to be legally alert in our litigious society, where innocent, straightforward questions can be misunderstood, twisted, and taken out of context.

Attorneys use sophisticated software programs to find what they need to establish or manipulate liability in court. Software exists to search emails for much more than obvious "hot words" (*tax liability, ISIS, fraud, the IRS, the SEC, loop-*

holes). These software programs can search for phrases that suggest someone is concerned about a problem: *"forced to take a leave of absence," "do it while he's on vacation," "serious concerns about this," "force her off the board," "that topic we discussed over lunch," "fight back," "can't let anyone get wind of this," "turn any questions about that situation over to me directly," "how would anyone find out?" "Be sure to delete this email." "What about the legality of this?"*

Such software can detect when the same report might have been sent to two different people (but with different transmittal emails). It can analyze a sudden change of writing style over someone's signature and trace traffic patterns between people. For example, these legal software programs can detect that you always transmit report X on the 17th of the month, but in October you delayed the report for three days. Why? Were you intentionally waiting until after the Big Meeting happened?

Such software can identify that you typically invite Joe, Haley, Jamil, Shawn, and Carmen to financial meetings. But in April you did not invite Shawn. Why not? Was that because the merger and declaration of bankruptcy were under discussion?

Imagine that in the case above about the auto manufacturing process, your coworker Curtis copied you on his email when he raised this question: *"Should we do more testing on the XYZ system before moving on to the next stage?"* Now you're "in the know" about the situation. There's a permanent email traffic record linking you to this information.

But let's say you didn't respond because you considered the question was really something for the engineers to work out among themselves. After all, you're just the sales guy. They copied you just as a courtesy in case there was a delay and the customer asked for a status about delivery dates. In court, the attorneys will ask you why you didn't take the "warning" seriously. Why no response? Were you concerned that the increased cost for more testing would lower company profits and your sales commission? (Note how the innocent question has morphed into a "warning.")

You get the idea. If a nasty lawsuit develops, consider what such emails and traffic patterns when discussed in court could do to damage your integrity. Even if you feel certain that your email does not address a legal matter, consider what its contents might do to keep you awake at night.

For example, let's say that as you're negotiating for a raise, you ask to take on additional responsibilities to correct "problems and inefficiencies" in your department and division. Later, imagine yourself unexpectedly being called into a C-suite meeting to explain your "derogatory" comments about the company in your email referencing "problems and inefficiencies."

The conclusion here: Be legally alert. Keep your meeting dates, distribution lists, writing style, and communication habits consistent. Consistency counts to establish your integrity and prove the lack of shenanigans.

You wouldn't be the first person to lose a job—or a lawsuit—over innocent email blunders.

Be legally alert. Keep your meeting dates, distribution lists, writing style, and communication habits consistent. Consistency counts to prove the lack of shenanigans.

LET SENSITIVE EMAILS COOL OFF

As the writer, you're a poor judge of the tone of your email. If in doubt about whether to hit SEND, don't. Let your email cool off in the draft folder overnight. If a response is urgent, get a colleague to review a draft (not forwarded to them!) or read it to them over the phone for feedback on the tone.

If your impatience gets the better of you and you send the flaming sword first, you've just melted down and flamed out while everyone watched.

If you've hastily sent a flame that you regret, one option is to recall the email before the recipient reads it. Open your SENT ITEMS folder and then open your flaming message. Next, go to ACTIONS and click on "RECALL THIS MESSAGE." If your message hasn't been read, you can then choose to delete or replace the message with a new one.

But don't count on this recall plan as a backup for your impulsiveness: Although Microsoft Outlook may tell you "No recipients have reported reading this message," it could be that your readers don't use Outlook. Or your readers may not be on your server. In fact, a website devoted to Outlook issues (https://www.msoutlook.info/question/recall-a-sent-message) notes that because of the necessary conditions it "hardly ever works as you want it to." This author suggests another workaround: Change your settings to delay the transmission of messages by a set time. That delay will give you time to "think it over" and delete the message if you have a change of heart.

HONOR COPYRIGHTS AND UNDERSTAND WHAT EMAILS YOUR ORGANIZATION OWNS

The creator of a document holds the copyright—unless it's a "work for hire." That is, if you're writing emails while earning a salary, your emails are "work for hire." Your organization owns them.

From time to time, you probably receive emails from colleagues outside your organization that contain items not exactly work-related: chain letters, jokes, cartoons, a slide of startling statistics, a YouTube video, even a coworker's personal rant, right?

If a coworker emails you an ezine story, speech script, or report without the copyright notification, beware. The sender may have cut and pasted it into their email without the original source, but that doesn't mean the original document wasn't copyrighted. Actually, it would be rare if the original writing was *not* copyright-protected.

You don't have the right to pass on these copyrighted

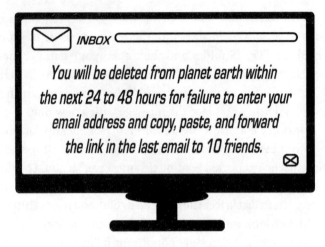

INBOX

You will be deleted from planet earth within the next 24 to 48 hours for failure to enter your email address and copy, paste, and forward the link in the last email to 10 friends.

You're liable for what you forward
on company equipment and systems.

items someone sends without permission of the owner. If you didn't create them, you don't own them and can't pass them on legally.

A speaker colleague reports that one of his growing revenue streams is settlement money collected as he prosecutes people and companies for unauthorized use of data and information lifted from his ezines, blogs, and website articles.

Ignorance is not a defense. If you forward documents sent to you by colleagues, you're liable for copyright infringement. Infringement is a criminal act that results in more than a hand slap.

Many email users mistakenly think their use (forwarding) of a copyrighted white paper, video clip, report template, or ezine is permitted under the Fair Use clause of copyright law. They argue that no one is paying them for the document. And often, they have noble purposes for the material—training others or educating the public for charitable causes.

But the Fair Use clause in copyright law doesn't necessarily permit such use. Four criteria determine fair use—and *all four* criteria must be met in each situation.

1. Is the purpose of the challenged use commercial or nonprofit (educational, a health warning, a safety prevention alert)? (If you're making money from someone else's intellectual property, that's going to be a problem.)

2. Is the work the original author's unique expression or just facts available to anyone? (Facts cannot be copyrighted. But someone's unique presentation or organization of those facts can be copyrighted and protected.)

3. How substantial is the length of the copied work in comparison to the whole document? (3 percent of the whole? 25 percent of the whole? 40 percent of the whole?) (If you're quoting two sentences of someone's 2,000-word white paper, they might not challenge you as long as you credit them as your source. But use three words of someone's six-line tag phrase, and you'll likely have an infringement lawsuit on your hands.)

4. Does the effect of your use reduce the value of the original work to the author? Would your use deprive the author of potential income? (A "yes" answer here should tell you that you're about to face a big fine.)

A court will consider all four issues before determining infringement and assessing penalties. To repeat: Fair use means you have to pass muster on *all four* criteria. Rarely in ordinary email traffic will you be legally free to forward copyrighted material. Even if you don't claim ownership of the ideas or words and even if you acknowledge other sources, you may be liable for infringement.

On copyright infringement . . .
ignorance is not a defense. . . .
It's a bellyache and a bulldozer
over your bank account and career.

Not only will the author be on your trail but likely so will others who have paid licensing fees for the material you are using and forwarding. Ignorance is not bliss. It's a bellyache and a bulldozer over your bank account and career.

USE EOM AND FYI IN THE SUBJECT LINE

The acronym EOM stands for End of Message. Inserted at the end of a subject line, this >EOM allows readers to skim their inbox and read only the subject line without even opening the email.

> **Subject Line:** *Barrett Meeting on 7/8 Cancelled;*
> *They Lost Contract >EOM*

Readers can rest assured that they got the entire message—clearly—and file, forward, or delete as appropriate.

FYI (For Your Information) inserted in the subject line allows the same courtesy: A short-cut decision about filing, forwarding, or deleting:

> **Subject Line:** *FYI: All Reviews on Model B298*
> *Collected—No Action Needed*

With such routine consideration for your reader's time, your reputation for productivity will likely soar.

IDENTIFY STANDARD RESPONSE TIMES

Eighty percent of the participants in the UNC survey typically expect readers to respond to "important" emails within four hours or less; 59 percent expect a response within an hour or less.

What's the standard response time expected in your organization: One hour? Four hours? Twenty-four hours? Are there exceptions? If so, what? If you don't know, find out from your organizational leader. (If you are the leader, communicate the standard to your team.) Protect your personal brand by living up to the expectations set. Slow responses suggest many things—most of them negative.

- You're overwhelmed and can't keep up with the pace.
- You're puzzled by the decision or action required.
- Your system of handling daily inquiries is ineffective.
- You have a staffing problem.
- The situation, decision, or project is unimportant to you.
- You need to gather more information or input before replying.
- You need time to deliberate before responding.

Can you routinely afford to be considered the bottleneck?

FORWARD PERSONAL COMMENTS ONLY WITH PERMISSION

At the family reunion, what do you think of Aunt Bessie who has already "let everyone in on a little secret" that is not really hers to share? In other words, she shares the "secret" before the happy couple gets a chance to announce their engagement, before your niece gets to tell that she won a part in the school play, before your brother announces he's moving to Singapore for an exciting new job?

Enough said. At work, let the owner of the news, policy, or announcement share it if they're so inclined.

FOLLOW THE RULES OF ETIQUETTE

You don't just show up at a wedding without being invited. Nor would you tell a party host that you had a lousy time and insist they never invite you again. Neither do you barge into a LinkedIn or Facebook group and start posting insults about other members—or at least, not for long. The administrator or other members will quickly oust you.

Almost every activity has social rules of acceptable behavior. Break them at your peril. Emailing differs in only one way—the consequences can be stiffer. Fail to follow the generally accepted rules on a daily basis and your reputation may be ruined until you move to a new position or organization and begin to interact with a new group of colleagues.

So learn what's expected in your culture:

Respond to emails within the expected timeframe.

Acknowledge receipt of an email. If you can't respond with all the information someone wants, at least let them know you got their email and when to expect a complete answer. Otherwise, you're leaving them to wonder if the email went into your spam file or cyberspace. You're setting yourself up to get reminders at the most inopportune times.

Avoid using the "return receipt requested" feature unless your aim is to document an enemy's failure to perform.

EVALUATE THE PROS AND CONS OF EMOJIS

The use of emojis elicits strong reactions among a diverse audience. Two decades ago, in my earlier book on business writing (*E-Writing: 21st-Century Tools for Effective Communication*), I wrote that emoticons were unacceptable in formal business writing.

While that's still true in *formal* emails going outside the organization, emojis have gained general acceptance in internal emails to colleagues. Emoji use in social media and texting has "overflowed" into the email channel. In fact, email marketers in some industries report higher response rates when they use emoticons.

But that's not to say you should use them routinely in your emails. Consider the pros and cons:

The Pros in Using Emojis

- Fast (a shortcut way to express yourself)
- Fun (adds playfulness; cute, tongue-in-cheek, ironic, sarcastic)
- Friendly (adds a touch of personality)

The Cons in Using Emojis

- Immature/childish (as judged by many readers)
- Inappropriately lighthearted for the situation or topic (insensitive)
- Ambiguous (What does the expression mean exactly? Select your emoticon carefully.)

Bottom line: Give serious thought before using lighthearted emojis rather than expressing yourself in words.

SWIM IN THEIR CHANNEL, DON'T SWITCH

It's not all about you. While you likely prefer one communication channel over the others, most other people have their favorite channel as well

In the UNC survey, respondents in all age groups (Millennials through Traditionalists) listed email communication as the most important method of communication for their work (48 percent of the respondents). Face-to-face communication ranked as the second most important method (18 percent). Phone calls were rated as the third most important way to communicate (17 percent), with texting as the fourth most important communication channel (7 percent). Instant messaging was significantly less important than other forms in all groups (ranked only slightly higher than video conferencing).

Some like the speed and ease of texting while others dislike texting because texts can't be saved in their database and linked to a client record. Others prefer email because their messages run long, and typing on their phone becomes too tedious. Some like to phone for a quick back-and-forth discussion in real time to make a decision. Still others send a message through social media and are fine waiting for a few days until they get a response.

Obviously, it's a temptation to move the discussion over to your preferred channel because it's convenient and comfortable for you. But unless you're the C-suite executive who

Avoid annoying coworkers and clients
by chasing them from channel to channel.

gets to call the shots, don't. Switching channels creates a ripple in the rapport you've built with that colleague or client.

To someone who finds the new channel uncomfortable, switching in the middle of a discussion communicates the same message as "You live in the wrong neighborhood" or "You drive the wrong kind of car."

AVOID SENDING DUPLICATE MESSAGES
IN MULTIPLE CHANNELS

Granted, some people can be infuriatingly slow to respond to email. Just because email allows you to respond 24/7 at your convenience doesn't mean you should. One person whom I've corresponded with through the years admits to being "the world's worst about responding." I agree with her self-assessment. Routinely, it takes her a couple of weeks to answer an email. Quite often, a couple of months!

When you must interact with these colleagues, you're tempted to leave multiple messages in all channels: text, email, phone, social media. Most often, their reaction is annoyance.

If you're getting slow responses in one channel, find out where they are and go there. (In the case of my colleague, I discovered that she operates almost exclusively on social media.)

USE MULTIPLE CHANNELS TO COMMUNICATE
WITH A WIDESPREAD AUDIENCE

While it's usually best to avoid duplicate messages on multiple channels, here's the exception: When you need to communicate with a large audience, and they may not all be using the same channel.

In a survey of 1,200 US workers conducted by EmployeeChannel, Inc., workers at all levels reported that they desired the same thing: more frequent communication from their employer, specifically from their HR teams. Nearly half of the employees reported they felt "neutral, disagreed, or strongly disagreed" that the HR team's communication efforts made them feel more informed or engaged at work. And a whopping 75 percent of the respondents said that HR communicates with them "never or rarely" or only "sometimes."

Yet the corresponding HR teams and their organizations say they are firmly committed to open communication and invest huge time and effort in communicating with employees. Why the gap in perception and reality?

Sandy Yu, VP of marketing and product management at EmployeeChannel and author of the article published at TLNT.com, suggests this explanation for the gap: "Communications too often fail to reach employees."[4]

The study goes on to reveal other puzzling data—puzzling at least to those emailers who want to solve this problem. Those same employees who reported that they wanted more communication from their organization were adamant about the channel—about what they did *not* want.

- Only 16 percent wanted to receive an email
- Fewer than 12 percent wanted in-person meetings
- Only 5 percent wanted to be communicated with by phone

You can walk away with at least two conclusions from this study: (1) People say they want more communication, but they begrudge the time required. (2) People prefer different channels. No one size fits all.

So if you intend to push a message out to a wide audience, you'll need to use a multichannel approach to see that it reaches everyone.

CHOOSE THE APPROPRIATE CHANNEL WHEN THE CHOICE IS YOURS

Remember that email may not be the best channel for the message you're sending or the audience you want to reach. Evaluate both. Email is a good choice when:

- You need to communicate with a large number of people quickly.
- The message is not time-sensitive.
- You want to document what you sent and when (such as a file copy for legal reasons).
- The reader(s) may need the information for later reference—such as complex instructions.
- The reader may want to forward your complex details or information to others.

Email is a poor choice for communicating when:

- You need to negotiate details of a situation (deadlines, details, requests) that may change frequently as the discussion progresses. *[Talk.]*
- You want an immediate response. *[Either text or call.]*
- The message may be emotionally charged and the tone difficult to convey in writing. *[Either call or meet.]*
- You want to see the reaction to an emotional message to determine its effect. *[Meet.]*

- You want the recipient to have your message as a remembrance (commendation, anniversary, commemoration, recognition). *[Send a formal certificate, announcement, or letter.]*
- You want to create impact about the serious nature of a situation (a warning about termination, a threat of lawsuit). *[Write a formal letter.]*
- The information is highly confidential and/or could create legal liability. (Others can forward an email without your knowledge, alter or omit words, or change its meaning by dropping the email into a different context.) *[Meet.]*

■ ■ ■

Email can boost your productivity tremendously—but only if you manage it rather than let it lock you into poor communication habits. Now you have the keys to freedom. Run with them.

Your Next Steps

For more on this topic, go to
www.FasterFewerBetterEmails.com
to download *Your 10-Step Implementation Plan for Email Productivity* to help you "spread the word" throughout your organization. You'll also find a Discussion Guide and other learning resources.

Get Dianna's weekly blog mailed to your inbox by signing up at **www.BooherResearch.com/blog**.

This ezine provides ongoing practical tips on communication in all its forms—oral, written, interpersonal, and enterprise-wide. Topics frequently address leadership communication, executive presence, sales communication, customer service communication, and book writing and publishing.

Notes

1. Booher Research Institute study, completed in partnership with the Social Research Lab at the University of Northern Colorado, September 2018. A scientifically representative sampling of 311 knowledge workers among all age groups in the workforce, across 10 industries in the United States. Respondents can be further categorized as follows: 37.7 percent management, 28.8 percent have some management responsibilities, 33.4 percent have no management responsibilities.

2. Carleton Newsroom, "Carleton Study Finds People Spending a Third of Job Time on Email," Carleton Newsroom, April 20, 2017, https://newsroom.carleton.ca/archives/2017/04/20/carleton -study-finds-people-spending-third-job-time-email/; The Radicati Group, Inc. *Email Statistics Report, 2017–2021, Executive Summary*, www.Radicati.com; Dani-Elle Dubé, "This Is How Much Time You Spend on Work Emails Every Day, According to a Canadian Survey," *Global News*, April 21, 2017, https://global news.ca/news/3395457/this-is-how-much-time-you-spend-on -work-emails-every-day-according-to-a-canadian-survey/; Microsoft, *The Cost of Email Use in the Workplace: Lower Productivity and Higher Stress*, 2016, https://www.microsoft.com/en-us /research/publication/the-cost-of-email-use-in-the-workplace -lower-productivity-and-higher-stress/; Michael Chui, James Manyika, Jacques Bughin, et al., "The Social Economy: Unlocking Value and Productivity Through Social Technologies," McKinsey Global Institute Report, July 2016, http://www.mckinsey.com / industries/high-tech/our-insights/the-social-economy/.

3. J. Smallwood and J. W. Schooler, "The Restless Mind," *Psychological Bulletin* 132 (2006): 946–958, http://dx.doi.org/10.1037 /0033-2909.132.6.946.

4. Sandy Yu, "Engagement Woes? Try Improving How You Communicate with Workers," TLNT.com, July 5, 2018, https:// www.tlnt.com/engagement-woes-try-improving-how-you -communicate-with-workers/.

Bibliography

WEBSITES FOR QUOTATIONS
Brainy Quote. https://brainyquote.com.
Goodreads. https://www.goodreads.com.
The Quote Garden. http://www.quotegarden.com/.
"Quotes on Email." Wylie Communications. https://www
    .wyliecomm.com/writing-tips/online-communications
    /email/quotes-on-email/.
Wise Old Sayings. http://www.wiseoldsayings.com.

PUBLICATIONS
Ariely, Dan. "Email Notifications." http://danariely.com/2017/02/23
    /email-notifications/. Accessed August 2, 2018.
Booher, Dianna. *Booher's Rules of Business Grammar: 101 Fast
    and Easy Ways to Correct the Most Common Errors.* New York:
    McGraw-Hill, 2009.
———. *Clean Up Your Act!: Effective Ways to Organize Paperwork—
    And Get It Out of Your Life.* New York: Warner Books, 1992.
———. *Communicate Like a Leader: Connecting Strategically
    to Coach, Inspire, and Get Things Done.* Oakland, CA: Berrett-
    Koehler, 2017.
———. *E-Writing: 21st-Century Tools for Effective Communication.*
    New York: Simon and Schuster/Pocket Books, 2001.
———. *Good Grief, Good Grammar: The Business Person's Guide
    to Grammar and Usage.* New York: Ballentine, 1988.
Carleton Newsroom. "Carleton Study Finds People Spending a
    Third of Job Time on Email." Carleton Newsroom, April 20, 2017.
    https://newsroom.carleton.ca/archives/2017/04/20/carleton-study
    -finds-people-spending-third-job-time-email/.
Chui, Michael, James Manyika, Jacques Bughin, et al. *The Social
    Economy: Unlocking Value and Productivity Through Social
    Technologies.* McKinsey Global Institute Report, July 2012. http://
    www.mckinsey.com/industries/high-tech/our-insights/the-social
    -economy/. Accessed July 30, 2018.
Dubé, Dani-Elle. "This Is How Much Time You Spend on Work
    Emails Every Day, According to a Canadian Survey." *Global News,*

April 21, 2017. https://globalnews.ca/news/3395457/this-is-how
-much-time-you-spend-on-work-emails-every-day-according-to
-a-canadian-survey/. Accessed July 30, 2018.

Koren, Marina. "The Most Honest Out-of-Office Message."
The Atlantic, June 11, 2018. https://www.theatlantic.com
/technology/archive/2018/06/out-of-office-message-email/562394/.
Accessed August 2, 2018.

Microsoft. *The Cost of Email Use in the Workplace: Lower Productivity
and Higher Stress*. 2016. https://www.microsoft.com/en-us
/research/publication/the-cost-of-email-use-in-the-workplace
-lower-productivity-and-higher-stress/. Accessed July 30, 2018.

Radicati Group, Inc. *Email Statistics Report, 2017–2021, Executive
Summary*. www.Radicati.com. Accessed August 2, 2018.

Robinson, Kent Alan. *Unsend: Email, Text, and Social Media Disasters
. . . and How to Avoid Them*. 2016.

Shipley, David, and Will Schwalbe. *Send: The Essential Guide to Email
for Office and Home*. New York: Knopf, 2007.

Smallwood, J., and J. W. Schooler. "The Restless Mind." *Psychological Bulletin* 132 (2006): 946–958. http://dx.doi.org/10.1037
/0033-2909.132.6.946. Accessed August 2, 2018.

Song, Mike, Vicki Halsey, and Tim Burress. *The Hamster Revolution:
How to Manage Your Email Before It Manages You*. Oakland, CA:
Berrett-Koehler, 2007.

Yu, Sandy. "Engagement Woes? Try Improving How You Communicate with Workers." TLNT.com. July 5, 2018. https://www.tlnt
.com/engagement-woes-try-improving-how-you-communicate
-with-workers/. Accessed July 5, 2018.

Acknowledgments

As always, I owe a big debt of gratitude to my clients through the years for sharing their stories and email samples with me.

Thanks to Dr. Josh Packard, Megan Bissell, and the staff of the Social Research Lab at the University of Northern Colorado for conducting the survey among email users across many industries and at all levels of white-collar workers. Their input was invaluable in discerning the latest email reader experiences and expectations, especially regarding the technology used and security issues.

Next, I'd like to thank early reviewers of the manuscript for their insightful comments: Judy Gilleland, Sarah Modlin, Tobin O'Donnell, Vernon Rae, Frappa Stout, and Joseph Webb.

Finally, a very special thanks to all the team at Berrett-Koehler, especially my editor, Neal Maillet. It would be hard to find a nicer team of folks to work with in publishing a book.

Index

abbreviations and acronyms: audience consideration in use of, 59; EOM and FYI use in professional emails, 112

absences, email handling after, 18–19

actions: avoiding multiple, 38–39; examples of buried/unclear, 30, 32, 34; in MADE Format™, 27, 31, 33, 35, 37; providing specific follow-up, 27, 41, 79, 80

adjectives, 61–62

adverbs, 61–62

alerts: decluttering strategies on, 19; scheduling tools for, 8–9

announcements, 17–18, 113

antivirus/anti-malware software, 99–100

apostrophes, 53, 76

attachments: as message, 29; as security risk, 99; in signature blocks, 51

audience: analysis of, 22–26; communication channels for widespread, 117–118; consideration for, with abbreviations/acronyms, 59; greetings matching, 47–48; style and tone in relation to, 79

automatic retrieval, 19

bad-news emails, 29, 36

Bcc (blind copy) emails, 40

blog, 121

Booher Research Institute, 3, 123n.1

brain dumps, 21–22

brevity, 53; considerations with, 49–50; editing for appropriate, 5, 59–65; of signature block, 51. *See also* conciseness

Brogan, Chris, 7

calendaring software, 8–9

Cc emails: appropriate use of, 40; removing oneself from, 16–17; responding to, 15–16

Cicero, 53

clarity: climactic sentence for, 56–57; of dates in emails, 13; editing for, 54–59; effect of punctuation on, 72–74; font aiding in, 13, 50, 56; with lists, 54; how lack of clarity affects reputation, 2; in pronoun references, 55–56; subject lines edited for, 58

climactic sentence, 56–57

closings. *See* signature block; sign-offs/closings

commas, 53–54, 72–75

communication channels: duplicate messages, 116–117; face-to-face preference for, 115, 117–119; selecting appropriate, 118–119; staying within, 115–116; for widespread audience, 117–118

conciseness: active voice for, 60–61; editing for, 5, 59–65; example of, 64; and "little-word" padding, 61; verb use for, 60, 68

contact information, 13, 50–51

copyright infringement/protection, 105, 109–112

credibility: email influence on, 2, 25, 53

dates: clarity of, 13; in folder and file names, 91; of meetings, 108

deadlines, responding to, 12–13

debit card scam, 93–95

decluttering strategies, 5; for Cc emails, 15–17; for dealing with email upon reading, 9–10; for distribution lists, 14–15; for email alerts, 19; for e-zines, 18; for inbox, 18–19; for "piling on" responses, 10–11; for receipt acknowledgments, 12–13; for reminder and follow-up emails, 9–10, 12–14; and "reply all"

About the Author

Dianna Booher's lifework has centered around communication in all its forms: oral, written, interpersonal, and enterprise-wide. As author of forty-eight books, translated into sixty foreign language editions (as well as numerous other coauthored books), she has traveled the globe, talking with clients and organizations on six continents about communication challenges they face at work and at home. Despite cultural differences, two things remain the same: Communication is the basic business act. And communication either cements or destroys personal and work relationships.

Improving communication skills, habits, and attitudes dramatically changes life—for an individual, a family, an organization, and a nation. Dianna considers that an exciting and rewarding business and personal goal.

Based in the Dallas–Fort Worth Metroplex, her firm, Booher Research Institute, works with organizations to help them communicate clearly and with leaders to expand their influence by a strong executive presence.

During her more than three decades at Booher Research Institute and earlier at Booher Consultants, she and her team have provided communication training programs, coaching, and consulting to governmental agencies and more than one-third of the Fortune 500 organizations.

Successful Meetings magazine has named Dianna to its list of "21 Top Speakers for the 21st Century." The National Speakers Association has awarded her its highest honor: induction into the Speaker Hall of Fame. She is also listed among the "Global Gurus Top 30 Communicators" and Richtopia's "Top 200 Most Influential Authors in the World."

The national media frequently interview Dianna for opinions on communication issues: *Good Morning America, USA*

Today, Forbes, The Wall Street Journal, Fast Company, Success, Entrepreneur, Investor's Business Daily, FOX, CNN, Bloomberg, NPR, *The New York Times,* and *The Washington Post.*

She also blogs regularly for *Forbes* and *The CEO Magazine.*

Dianna holds a master's degree in English literature from the University of Houston.

For more information about Dianna's work and her speaking engagements, visit www.BooherResearch.com.

How to Work with Dianna Booher and Booher Research Institute

KEYNOTES AND CONSULTING

If you have any of these challenges or goals, Dianna and her team can help.

- "Our people are working harder and longer hours. The email is killing us!"
- "Our next group of young leaders lack executive presence.
- "Our salespeople make face-to-face presentations and they need more polish."
- "People say there's no communication around here, yet we send them plenty of information, hold regular staff meetings, and update our intranet. We have no idea what they mean!"
- "We get far too many customer complaints about our communication. It's costing us time and money to respond."

PERSONAL COACHING ON EXECUTIVE PRESENCE, SALES PRESENTATIONS, OR BOOK WRITING AND PUBLISHING

- We will design an individual coaching program to fit your needs and schedule.
- If your speakers for an upcoming meeting are experts in their field but are not necessarily

engaging speakers, we can help them structure and deliver a dynamic presentation.

- If you're an entrepreneur, CEO, consultant, or other professional wanting to establish your credentials by writing and publishing a book with a major publisher, Dianna can coach you through that process. Go to www.GetYourBookPublished CoachingProgram.com.

After consulting and coaching executives at more than one-third of the Fortune 500 organizations, Dianna and her team have the research, expertise, and practical techniques and tools to help you reach your goals.

For More Information

Booher Research Institute, Inc.
817-283-2333
www.BooherResearch.com
clients@BooherResearch.com
Dianna.Booher@BooherResearch.com
www.FasterFewerBetterEmails.com

Please connect on your favorite social media channels.
@DiannaBooher
LinkedIn.com/In/DiannaBooher
Facebook.com/DiannaBooher
YouTube.com/DiannaBooher
www.BooherResearch.com/blog

Go to **www.FasterFewerBetterEmails.com** to download
Your 10-Step Implementation Plan for Email Productivity
to "spread the word" in your organization. You'll also find
a Discussion Guide and other learning resources.

Also by Dianna Booher

Creating Personal Presence
Look, Talk, Think, and Act Like a Leader

Personal presence can help you lead a meeting, a movement, or an organization. Presence is not something you're born with—anyone can learn these skills and traits. Award-winning speaker and consultant Dianna Booher shows how to master dozens of small and significant things that work together to convey presence.

Paperback, 216 pages, ISBN 978-1-60994-011-9
PDF ebook, ISBN 978-1-60994-012-6
ePub ebook ISBN 978-1-60994-013-3
Digital audio, ISBN 978-1-5230-8265-0

Communicate Like a Leader
Connecting Strategically to Coach, Inspire, and Get Things Done

Dianna Booher wants to prevent micromanagement before it happens by providing you with the right leadership communication skills. Grounded in extensive research, this book offers practical guidelines to help professionals think, coach, speak, write, and negotiate strategically to deliver results.

Paperback, 208 pages, ISBN 978-1-62656-900-3
PDF ebook, ISBN 978-1-62656-901-0
ePub ebook ISBN 978-1-62656-902-7
Digital audio, ISBN 978-1-62656-904-1

BK° Berrett–Koehler Publishers, Inc.
www.bkconnection.com   800.929.2929

Berrett–Koehler
Publishers

Berrett-Koehler is an independent publisher dedicated to an ambitious mission: *Connecting people and ideas to create a world that works for all.*

Our publications span many formats, including print, digital, audio, and video. We also offer online resources, training, and gatherings. And we will continue expanding our products and services to advance our mission.

We believe that the solutions to the world's problems will come from all of us, working at all levels: in our society, in our organizations, and in our own lives. Our publications and resources offer pathways to creating a more just, equitable, and sustainable society. They help people make their organizations more humane, democratic, diverse, and effective (and we don't think there's any contradiction there). And they guide people in creating positive change in their own lives and aligning their personal practices with their aspirations for a better world.

And we strive to practice what we preach through what we call "The BK Way." At the core of this approach is *stewardship,* a deep sense of responsibility to administer the company for the benefit of all of our stakeholder groups, including authors, customers, employees, investors, service providers, sales partners, and the communities and environment around us. Everything we do is built around stewardship and our other core values of *quality, partnership, inclusion,* and *sustainability.*

This is why Berrett-Koehler is the first book publishing company to be both a B Corporation (a rigorous certification) and a benefit corporation (a for-profit legal status), which together require us to adhere to the highest standards for corporate, social, and environmental performance. And it is why we have instituted many pioneering practices (which you can learn about at www.bkconnection.com), including the Berrett-Koehler Constitution, the Bill of Rights and Responsibilities for BK Authors, and our unique Author Days.

We are grateful to our readers, authors, and other friends who are supporting our mission. We ask you to share with us examples of how BK publications and resources are making a difference in your lives, organizations, and communities at www.bkconnection.com/impact.

Dear reader,

Thank you for picking up this book and welcome to the worldwide BK community! You're joining a special group of people who have come together to create positive change in their lives, organizations, and communities.

What's BK all about?

Our mission is to connect people and ideas to create a world that works for all.

Why? Our communities, organizations, and lives get bogged down by old paradigms of self-interest, exclusion, hierarchy, and privilege. But we believe that can change. That's why we seek the leading experts on these challenges—and share their actionable ideas with you.

A welcome gift

To help you get started, we'd like to offer you a **free copy** of one of our bestselling ebooks:

www.bkconnection.com/welcome

When you claim your **free ebook**, you'll also be subscribed to our blog.

Our freshest insights

Access the best new tools and ideas for leaders at all levels on our blog at ideas.bkconnection.com.

Sincerely,

Your friends at Berrett-Koehler

Certified

Corporation